"This is a great read for anyone seeking to make a positive impact in their world while still staying true to themselves. Cindie lays out the blueprint that is easy to read, but sometimes hard to follow: Work hard, trust your instincts, have the courage to do what you know is right, and don't look to others for validation; rather, find it in the deeper contentment rooted in a job well done."

—Mark Cooper
President, Seasons 52 and Bahama Breeze

"**Shards in My Hair** is packed with valuable real-life career lessons of experience, from entry-level to the boardroom, demonstrating important leadership insights in action. Cindie shares her journey in a thoroughly engaging, transparent, and humble way, laced with humor and hard-earned wisdom."

—Fraser Clark
Leadership Consultant/Executive Coach, ARC Leadership Associates

"In a world where everything looks easy from the outside-in, Jamison gets real about the mess that is life and the fascinating journey that led a single mom to the top of the business world."

—Kimberly Simpson
General Counsel, National Association of Corporate Directors

"Cindie Jamison's highly entertaining and informative book is more than a map for future female executives (though it is that). Combine the ingredients of hard work, perseverance, and a sense of humor with universal advice of how to succeed in the executive suite and boardroom and you have a winning book for everyone."

—Jane Howze
Managing Director, The Alexander Group (national executive search firm)

"Unfiltered, witty, and refreshingly honest, **Shards in My Hair** pulls back the curtain on what it really takes to succeed in the corporate world. With humor, vulnerability, and sharp insight, Cindie Jamison shares the highs, lows, and absurdities of her journey, making this a must read for anyone navigating leadership, career pivots, or personal growth. Equal parts hilarious and empowering, this is the no-BS guide to success you didn't know you needed."

—Maya Tubic
Owner, I Love My Assistant

"**Shards in My Hair: Lessons from Breaking the Glass Ceiling** is a gift to both seasoned leaders and emerging professionals—female and male! Brimming with sage and practical advice, Jamison narrates her multifaceted journey—professional and personal—with humor, tenderness, and authenticity. She manages to capture the essence of each lesson through a combination of experience, perspective, wisdom, and wry intellect. From dorm room to boardroom, and every stop in between, Jamison delivers insights into navigating a rocketing career as a single mom, handling stranger-than-fiction leadership challenges, and piloting the occasional existential crisis…all while allowing the reader to embrace the idea of being perfectly imperfect."

—Zoe Maloney
Chief Human Resource Officer, ODP Corporation

"Oh, how I wish I had read a book like this when I was a working mother coming up through the ranks of the business world. Cindie's authentic, humorous, and sometimes raw storytelling delivers an impactful message that left me with a sense of gratitude for her vulnerability in sharing such poignant lessons. Her pragmatic approach to handling a variety of personal and professional situations is something all women—and men—can learn from."

—Sarah King
Chief Human Resource Officer, Darden Restaurants

"**Shards in My Hair** is a great read for any professional looking to excel at work, at home, and 'do it all.' It's a constant balancing act and Cindie has been very successful in her journey because she's willing to ask for what she wants, try new things, and sometimes fail. This book shares her many successes, failures, and hilariously funny moments. She makes board directorships and C-suite roles seem more human and accessible."

—Lauren Werle
Vice President, Internal Audit, ODP Corporation

"In this hilarious and deeply personal life story, corporate America's powerful woman, Cindie Jamison, reveals a truthful account of the struggles, frustrations, and adversity she encountered during her rise to the top. In **Shards in My Hair** Jamison debunks the myth that success is easy. As a single mother of four boys and with a career marked by peaks and valleys, Jamison had plenty of chances to fail. Instead, her grit inspires readers everywhere, especially women, to trust that optimism and resilience is a key ingredient for success."

—Atlee Valentine-Pope
Lead Independent Director, Gibraltar Industries

Shards in My Hair

Shards in My Hair LLC
Chicago, Illinois

Published by Shards in My Hair LLC
Chicago, Illinois, USA

Print ISBN: 979-8-218671-32-7
ebook ISBN: 979-8-218671-33-4

This book is a memoir, based upon the author's best recollection of events. Some names and identifying characteristics have been changed for privacy; some events and dialogue may have been re-created or compressed.

Cover: Mandy Sloan Meador, illustrator and designer (sloanstitches.com)

To my sons' partners, Christina, Letty, Elleanore, and Hannah; to my stepdaughters, Michelle, Brooke, and Valentine; to my nieces, Jessica and Kate; and to my granddaughters, Annie, Sloane, Zuri, Isla, Sofia, and Parker: You are the future!

Contents

Foreword

Jeff Smith, Founder and CEO, Starboard Value

As an activist investor, I invest in good companies that are not achieving their potential and then become a catalyst to jump-start improved performance. While we often talk specifically about how a company should change its strategy to grow faster or improve efficiency to increase margins, the truth is: People run companies. Great management makes a big difference. A great board will provide better motivation, coaching, and leadership. In order to be successful as an activist investor, or probably any investor, or any businessperson, or any person, it is imperative to identify and appreciate great and talented people. I have been extremely fortunate. I work with some amazing people and have developed an enjoyable network of colleagues who have become trusted friends and advisors.

Through decades as an investor, I can say that it's not often you meet someone who refines your thinking on both strategy and leadership. My long-standing relationship with Cindie has been invaluable. Over the years, her insights have illuminated the very real challenges that many organizations face. Most importantly, not only can she identify the key issues, but she is an effective and collegial coach and communicator. Management and the board trust Cindie's insights and advice, making her invaluable for companies and shareholders.

What I didn't know, until I read this book, is the personal journey that took Cindie through the maturation curve to get to where she is today. It intrigued me and made me further appreciate the determination and grit that various experiences and challenges imbued in her from her early childhood, through juggling the complexities of being a single mother and a crisis CFO.

I have worked with Cindie in various settings since 2013. She has become an amazing advisor and friend. In addition to the improvements she has made inside companies, she has helped me improve my process and my communication. We have created some major successes, some terrific friendships, and improved companies and management teams. I have benefited from her wisdom, her humor, her persistence, and her perspective.

I know you will too.

Introduction: The Journey...

It all looks so easy from the outside. In the midst of either a night of internet surfing or sitting alone in your office after a particularly boring or blistering meeting, you google someone you've either met or recently heard of—just to see about their rise to the top, their net worth, and/or any juicy headlines regarding their success. Typically what you'll find, through a combination of LinkedIn, Facebook, Instagram, or Google, is something like this: They went to some prestigious school(s), typically for an MBA after undergrad, they worked in a succession of roles in recognizably named firms, they gained in title and stature along the way, perhaps they were "famous" for this or that (successful ad campaign, acquisition, turnaround, etc., etc.), and now they have either retired to the good life or they are currently sitting on a handful of public company boards. What, you wonder, is their secret? How do they make it look so easy? Why can't your career follow a similar path? Why are you finding it a) frustrating, b) tedious, or c) impossible to create a simple, linear, stimulating, progressing career path that promises the bright future you've worked so hard for and deserve?

Part of the problem in today's world of social media, in my opinion, is that the truth is often subjugated to the flamboyant—or perhaps to the mere convenient. In a world of pictures and soundbites, does anyone really have the interest or patience to digest the voluminous details actually involved with someone else's struggles and ultimate success? Is it catchy? No.

What it is, is a shame.

People's truths matter. People's characters are built through adversity, perseverance, frustration, and failure. Success is rarely attained without grit. As a friend of mine once told me, "A winner is just a loser who tried one more time."

I spent all of my life as an outsider—a kid who came from a family whose careers were in medicine. A college student supposedly headed for law school until a shockingly great GMAT score (taken while somewhat hungover) changed the trajectory. A woman in a grad school known (at the time) as a male, quantitative bastion. A young kid struggling to figure out a foreign and often cruel business world. An unexpectantly pregnant recent MBA grad—confined to bed rest for blood pressure issues months into her first big role, and a new mom trying to juggle said big role with a new infant . . . it goes on and on. But that is the stuff of the book and this is only the introduction.

Yet as an outsider, I had a keen interest in watching to learn. Watching whom to emulate to understand and predict success. Reading to gain insight into how to manage all of this. Engaging for years and years with peers, colleagues, friends, advisors, coaches, and bosses to grow and get better, smarter . . . to become "more." Guess what? Most of it didn't matter. None of it helped me find *me*. There were no easy answers from the outside. Maybe because everyone has to find their own way to figure out their own version of the truth and their own way forward—at least that is the prettiest explanation I can come up with.

A more cynical view, looking back from where I sit now? Maybe it's because it's hard to figure out the truth when you're busy living it—and everyone else is trying to figure it out too. Or (this is the darkest interpretation) maybe it's because honestly, most people suck at leadership, or don't want to be vulnerable enough to share their real experiences and struggles. It's impossible to find answers through those types of people.

For whatever reason, I struggled mightily. I was pretty much routinely alone, frustrated, worried, confused, confounded, and searching. In the midst of all of that, I was alternately smashingly successful, a complete failure, a great mom, a terrible mom, madly in love, getting divorced, feeling pretty great, and feeling like shit. I have had great bosses and terrible bosses. I have made amazing lifelong friends and had stunning betrayals. I have felt impostor syndrome more times than I can count. I still apologize too much—even for things I have had no hand in and no control over. And you would *never* guess where all of this brought me ...

I have been a turnaround chief financial officer of eight different companies, both public and private-equity owned. I have been chairman of the board of three public companies. I have raised four beautiful boys—all now adults doing amazing things.

I *am* the person you might google and think, "How was it so easy?"

This book exists for one reason only: Despite the fact that I am a very private person who keeps an incredibly low profile, I want to tell the truth. I look out from the boardrooms I sit in today and I see the struggle continue. And I see the lack of transparency—the triumph of ego over accuracy when people give advice to the ranks. I crave someone, anyone (even me!) to just tell it like it is or, rather, like it *was*. I suppose this is my legacy. It is not a glowing, linear success story. It is all of the "stuff" that happened (the hard, the awful, the funny, the absurd, the silly, the shocking) that brought me to the rarified place that I enjoy today.

And it is some of the lessons and conclusions that I can muster now—with the benefit of time and hindsight and some self-reflection. If there is anything unique that I bring to the party—different from other how-to books and memoirs—it is that through my unique career experience as both a turnaround CFO and as a board member, I saw the guts, the truth, of *many* different companies, across industries and at various levels of authority. I have seen it from the top down and the bottom up. And I have been able to compare and contrast the experiences. Through all of that, I have found that the struggles and the teachings have been remarkably consistent. And so I am fairly confident that they will resonate. I try to be real. I try to honestly own my own part in things. And I also call bullshit on a few others (names have been changed!).

My hope is that it demystifies success and the illusion that it's easy. I hope it helps anyone who sits alone and wonders why it's so hard and wonders if it's worth it. And most of all, since some of these truths might seem outrageous, I sincerely hope it makes you laugh, while also leaving you inspired.

Maybe it doesn't always have to be as hard as I found it to be.

Prologue

My Idol

Everyone knows of the perils of being a woman in Tudor England—especially if you were one of the six unlucky wives of Henry VIII. Most people immediately think of Anne Boleyn, mother of Elizabeth I . . . the lusty obsession of Henry, until she wasn't. Falsely accused of trumped-up charges and then beheaded. Or perhaps Catherine of Aragon—the long-suffering first wife—whose unwanted and hard-fought divorce brought on the Reformation. She died of (suspicious) "natural" causes to clear the way for his marriage to Anne Boleyn.

But the lesser-known story of Anne of Cleves is the one I am particularly drawn to. Henry's fourth wife was an arranged marriage after the death of his beloved Jane Seymour (mostly "beloved" because she produced a male heir shortly before her death from childbirth). Anne represented a political alliance with Germany—a Protestant nation when Henry was looking to solidify his separation from the Roman Church. He had only seen a portrait of her prior to agreeing to the marriage. Several other potential queens had turned him down . . . his reputation by this time well known as a tough guy to get along with.

Imagine Anne at twenty-four, sent by her brother, who had the authority to make marital decisions for her, to England for the very first time. She did not speak the language; she did not know the customs. I think we can all relate to that feeling of isolation and alienation in the corporate world; I know I have many times. I'm sure Anne had impostor syndrome big-time—not to mention the Sunday (Monday, Tuesday, Wednesday, Thursday, Friday, and Saturday) Scaries.

Henry thought he would surprise her and traveled to the port where her ship landed, dressed in disguise so that he could observe her anonymously. It did not go well. Allegedly he exclaimed to his entourage very loudly, "I like her not!" Yes, we've all had that first bad day on the job!

Much drama ensued and Henry tried every way he could think of to wiggle out of the marriage. But the contract had been signed and he was committed. They were married on January 6, 1540. Henry made it clear that he was not game for this union . . . refusing to consummate the marriage and going right back to playing the field. Anne was left alone and isolated, surrounded by ladies-in-waiting who were mostly spies for the king (as well as a few being his lovers).

I imagine Anne was terrified. Alone in a new country as a foreigner with no language skills, married to a brutal guy who not only seemingly couldn't stand her but was also known for disposing of wives in not-too-pleasant ways, she was isolated and without counsel. I'm sure she feared for her life.

Henry's minion, Thomas Cromwell (who was himself eventually executed, in part for arranging this marriage), was told to "solve the problem." So he approached Anne with the idea of an annulment, claiming the marriage was never consummated. Unlike some of Henry's other wives, she did not resist. She agreed immediately and proceeded to go away quietly, I'm sure immensely relieved to escape with her head intact.

But here's where it gets interesting. To start, Henry was uncharacteristically generous with her—himself relieved to escape fairly easily as well. They were divorced on July 12, 1540. He bestowed upon her several properties, including Hever Castle, Anne Boleyn's family estate. He gave her a large enough financial settlement so that she became one of the wealthiest women in England. And she gamely settled into her new role with the newly created (and quite absurd) title of "the king's beloved sister." The king, now romantically involved with Catherine Howard, a teenager he later executed, began inviting Anne to court and over time became quite fond of her. Eventually, he decreed that she was to be treated as the most important woman in England, only surpassed by his wife and legitimate children.

When the king died, Anne remained close with his children and accompanied Mary in her Coronation Procession and Service. She became quite popular with the general population. Her many servants consistently described her as a fair and generous employer. Anne never left England, her adopted home. And despite a terrifying start, she rose to the highest echelons of power and influence. She died at forty-one, most likely from cancer.

Why is she my idol? Well, first of all, she was pretty savvy in the midst of some pretty terrifying circumstances—way worse than any corporate politics I can think of. She played the long game. She didn't hold grudges, forgiving Henry and accepting his overtures of friendship despite the humiliation he had caused her. She built relationships with those in court and with her stepchildren despite being an outsider. She treated people fairly and held on to her dignity—even when many around her didn't. She did as much good in the world as she could, given the circumstances she was dealt, and did not complain. And in the end ... she won. Anne outlasted Henry and all of his other wives, leaving a fortune to those she loved and maintaining a front-row seat to the most important royal events of the day.

I'd say she was pretty badass—and someone we can all learn from! Let's see how the lessons we can learn apply in the corporate world today, shall we?

1

No Plan Is The Plan

*"When something goes wrong in your life, just yell
'PLOT TWIST!' ... and move on."*

—Anonymous

I t's really important that anyone in business (whether just starting out, or already on the journey) understands that things often don't go as planned. This can be a tough one, especially for the younger generation. There is a tendency in youth to believe that you have more control over factors influencing your success than you really do. Sure—hard work and smarts matter, but *so* many other factors come into play too, usually out of your control. And the arc of a career (and a life) is long. My story, as I have reflected on it while writing this book, is not without speed bumps. I was worried it might sound like it was written from a victim point of view in the beginning chapters. I thought about changing that. But it was, in fact, how it felt to me at the time. And I think it's important to capture that, because without capturing that element first, it is hard to appreciate the maturity and growth and perspective that came later. Growth is not easy and the business world can be pretty unforgiving. My evolving into a sea-soned professional required building muscles I never knew I had, or needed. And it is that story, in addition to the craziness and the chaos and the wide array of bosses and jobs that I have had, that I wanted to capture. And so, bear with me while we go back to the beginning and suffer through some of the embarrassing and humiliating episodes that challenged me to either grow and adapt, or opt out. It is from a place of privilege today that I am able to relive these, capture the learnings from them, and share them with you—in the hopes that my learning curve may shorten yours.

I was recently invited to a dinner celebrating scholarship students at Booth, the business school at the University of Chicago (my alma mater), and there were three second-year MBA scholarship students on stage taking questions. I was struck by how cocky they were. They were so sure they knew what they wanted, and what they wanted was so improbable. Most of them wanted private equity, and in my opinion, you bring nothing to private equity unless you've had a real job first . . . far from leading deal decisions, right out of grad school you will spend a hundred hours a week building models and crunching numbers for the real decision-makers. If you're lucky, you might get to sit in on a few meetings. Most wise up and opt out.

A man got up to make a statement, saying how he thought they were all so articulate. And they *were* very articulate—albeit naively optimistic. This inspired me to ask a question.

"I agree that you are all very articulate," I said. "You also strike me as being very sure of what you want to do. My question is, How do you think Booth has prepared you for the unexpected things that can occur in a career? The turns that you're not expecting, the twists that you can't anticipate and control."

All I got in return was blank stares. They didn't even understand the question.

"I don't plan to fail," said one of the students. And the others echoed various versions of the same assured, arrogant sentiment.

Afterward, three different people came up to me expressing that they loved my question, and while the students might not have understood me, they knew exactly what I was talking about. Those who are a couple of decades past their MBA know that life is often *not* linear, and the unexpected twists and turns can really throw you for a loop.

Certainly, nothing worked out the way I thought it would. But, when you're so busy thinking about today, and living with *today's* issues and *today's* challenges, you shouldn't have a lot of time to philosophize about where you want to be in twenty years. In other words: No plan *is* the plan. And it is a waste of time to think about ten or twenty, or even five years out … take it, if not one day at a time, at least one year at a time.

* * *

I grew up in suburban New Jersey, the youngest of three daughters of a small-town veterinarian and his homemaker wife. My parents were a true love story. They met in seventh grade and were together from that point on. They held hands wherever they went. I don't remember them ever fighting, or even having cross words. My father loved his profession and was proud of being a veterinarian. He was a kind and gentle man. He built up his practice and eventually did quite well due to some optical specialization that he mastered. He adored his daughters and spent time with us on the weekends, although he was gone working long hours during the week. He loved Frank Sinatra and whiskey sours and our ever-present golden retriever, Tawny.

My mother was more complex. She was the oldest of two girls in a strict religious family. Her father—of whom I only have vague memories—was an odd, distant, disinterested man. He did not believe in education for women and sent both her and her sister to trade schools. She did not like her father at all and often said that my father "saved" her. From the moment they married, she devoted her life to taking care of him. Her upbringing left her without a good parenting role model and also left two indelible marks on her: She insisted that her daughters be educated, and she had social aspirations to be "better" than her upbringing. This made her somewhat snobbish, even if it had a strong undertone of insecurity. She used to tell me, "You can be anything in the world—a president, a Supreme Court justice, or an astronaut," which was remarkable in that day and time. She expected a lot of me and she invested a lot in me.

It is due to my mother's complex influence that some of my earliest characteristics developed. She could also be quite critical, and I became an insecure overachiever, as I've come to appreciate many of my peers today are—or were—on their way up. I was driven by seeking approval, but in doing so, I made myself busier and busier—always striving for that smile, that nod, that compliment. I got her attention when I accomplished things or won prizes—but somehow it was never enough. I felt alone and I felt like I had to figure out things by myself. She was too sheltered and immature to really offer much parenting. She was not warm or affectionate. Yet, contradictorily, I felt "overloved" when it came to my accomplishments—because they became *her* accomplishments. I felt that I was too important to her. Failure became too scary to contemplate.

Despite it all, my childhood wasn't unpleasant. We were financially very comfortable. I was sent to the best schools and I never once felt unsafe or unloved. My sisters were significantly older than me—seven and eleven years older—and so I identified as an only child. My oldest sister got married and left college at nineteen (she completed both undergraduate and graduate school later in life), breaking my mother's heart at the time. My middle sister finished college but followed a boy there (her future husband, then ex-husband), also disappointing my mother. By the time I was alone in the house with my parents, from roughly ten years old on, all of my mother's social aspirations and frustrated ambitions were trained on me. But that had a lot of upsides; my parents had the money to not only send me to private school, but pay for my lessons in all kinds of random things: piano, ballet, ice-skating, voice, tennis. I was busy. Learning to live with the pace and the pressure was pretty easy for me—and I got used to juggling a lot of competing priorities. I loved school and studying, and reading was my escape from a pretty quiet life.

My parents were both introverts and had virtually no social life. I, on the other hand, would hear the ticking of the clocks throughout the house and dream of going somewhere—*anywhere*. I longed to see the world and experience things. I felt so trapped and wondered why my friends' families traveled to interesting places and spent time going to events and seeing the sights in and around the city. A few times I even cut school and headed into the city with a friend or two to walk around. I loved the pace and the energy. To this day I am truly an urban girl.

Intellectual pursuits became my escape route. I devoured books in my middle school years, attracted to biographies of strong women. I would go on binges and read every book I could find on famous women: Florence Nightingale, Edith Cavell, Jane Addams, Annie Oakley, Amelia Earhart, Marie Curie. With each literary "friend" (always women!), I would dive into their lives completely—dreaming about them, imagining their day-to-day life, and applauding their accomplishments. I am sure that this innate curiosity revealed some longing on my part to be parented and also to be guided toward a life of ambition. I was looking for female role models, and in doing so, I learned a lot about the determination and grit that it took those women to achieve their dreams. It also gave me an appreciation for the head start I had in life coming from a place of privilege, because many of the women I studied came from far more obscure backgrounds than I. I did not want to waste it. I also think it helped me immensely, and not only from a role model standpoint. According to Services to Schools National Library, "'Reading for pleasure is more closely associated with intrinsic motivation, it is reading that children do for themselves at their own pace, with whom they choose and in their own way.' . . . Research shows that reading for pleasure boosts academic achievement, and provides a foundation for critical, digital and information literacy."

In high school, I was a mixture of high achiever and party girl—an interesting balance that has lasted. I got good grades, and I had student leadership positions. I was voted "Most Likely to Succeed." Yet, I recognized that I felt more alive when I was social. Between junior and senior years of high school, I was invited to join a few friends who were going to live and work on Martha's Vineyard for the summer. We found an adorable rental right in the heart of Edgartown, and one of the girls had connections for us to get jobs on the island. Well, the jobs that materialized turned out to be housekeeping for a large hotel, not the waitressing job I had mentioned to my parents. They were not amused. I remember my mother saying, "No daughter of mine is going to clean toilets," and I was forced to pull out of the summer plans. But it is interesting how small episodes like this can have a BIG impact later on.

My parents let me visit my friends at the end of the summer—they had had a fabulous time exploring one of the most beautiful islands in the world and babysitting for James Taylor and Carly Simon in their off-hours. I was green with envy! I went to visit and I went for a run around the town—ending the run on a road that goes by the Harborview Hotel and looks out to the Edgartown Lighthouse. I remember vividly thinking to myself: "They won't take this away from me—I will come back here someday." And, in fact, I owned a home there for ten years, my oldest son got engaged there, and my husband and I got married there—coincidentally at the very hotel where I was going to be a maid. Martha's Vineyard has become a staple in our family and, as a friend once commented, my "wound-licking place." But my resentment at my parents for taking that away from me lingered.

In senior year of high school, I discovered that Duke University had a January freshman program. At the time, it was used as a deferral plan—kids who were accepted were randomly selected to start in January following their high school graduation instead of September. I'm not sure why or how they were selected, but I approached my high school guidance counselor and asked, "Why can't I try to go early instead of later?" I had the grades. I had enough credits to graduate and it seemed like an intriguing idea. I am not sure to this day why I was so impatient. I suppose it had to do with that boredom and that desire to go out and gain more experiences than I felt I was getting in suburban New Jersey. I wanted to grow and explore and I suppose I wanted some independence from my mother as well after the previous summer. Once Duke accepted me—the first-ever "early January admission"—I packed up my bags over Christmas break of senior year and headed to Durham, North Carolina. I was finally starting my adventure. I was off on my own!

While my father cried while driving away from me, I felt nothing but relief and excitement. I had no idea how crazy and complicated my journey would be—but I was "all in!"

* * *

Once at Duke it became obvious to me—as it does to so many—that the world was a lot larger, more complicated, and more competitive than I was used to. Coming from a small, private girls' school, all of the leadership positions—whether in student government, the arts, or sports, obviously went to girls. And there was not a lot of competition. At Duke, almost everyone I met was an overachiever. The intellectual capacity and curiosity level was higher than I had ever experienced. And the guys seemed to get the leadership roles. It was a new world. It took me a while to adjust.

At first, I struggled to find a niche. I actually struggled through most of Duke to find my identity. Academically I was very well prepared. Getting good grades came easily. Before I headed off to school, my parents had made it clear that they expected me to head into one of the professions, with graduate school being a clear destination. But they didn't have much advice that was practical unless it involved med school or vet school—neither of which were a fit for me.

Before college, my father attempted to turn me into the next family veterinarian . . . it didn't go well. I learned that I am squeamish around blood and gore—so I was going to have to find an alternative! My dad had suggested law school as a good goal, so without any understanding of what a legal career entailed, I stacked my schedule with political science and history courses.

I left for the summer after my first college semester feeling pretty proud of myself for navigating an unchartered course, and doing pretty darn well at it. But when I went home to "officially" graduate from high school, it was a rude awakening. I had so been looking forward to it, but there was a strange discomfort between me and the other kids—I had crossed the chasm and was already experiencing what they wouldn't start until September. I learned that there can be dissonance when you move on ahead of other people, and it felt like I was "different." It was a huge disappointment and probably the first time in my young life that I learned you "can't go back." I had also missed the "senior year spring," when all kinds of fun things occurred and people bonded together before leaving for college. I was a fish out of water. I'm guessing I probably talked a lot about my college escapades as a way of socializing and that probably created even more of a wedge. Looking back, I am sad and sorry that I did that to myself, but I also learned a valuable lesson . . . leaving friends behind is hard, but as someone later told me, "If you aren't losing friends at some points in your life, then you aren't growing."

The biggest blow came at the graduation ceremony itself. Poised to win at least some academic awards before I left, it honestly never crossed my mind that leaving early would disqualify me. Since no one had ever done this early-college thing before, there was no rulebook. As I sat at the ceremony and watched as all of the awards went to others, I gazed out at my mother in the audience and saw she was crying. I had disappointed her. Looking back on it, it seems pretty minor. But at the time it was very upsetting, especially to my mother, who told me her summer was "ruined" by it. I wrote a letter to the school asking why I was disqualified and got an incredibly snarky letter back from the principal. The only line I recall specifically was that he wrote, "You simply cannot have your cake and eat it too." Fair enough (even if not the nicest way to communicate with an eighteen-year-old), but I would say that the value of setting expectations in advance was impressed upon me, and I never forgot the shock and surprise of that day. Again ... unintended consequences.

As I reflect on my sophomore and junior years at Duke, I see that I was exposed to many new things—and yet, there was also a growing sense of dissonance, which lasted for years. I didn't really "fit" anywhere. In a way that was kind of fun; I would party with the partiers, and I could study with the nerds. I chose not to join a sorority because I thought the clubby principal of it was sort of stupid, yet I was actively involved as a "little sister" to my boyfriend's fraternity. I could be a Northerner but feel like a Southerner. But the flip side of all of that was a certain loneliness and boredom.

The opportunity came to leave Duke and go to Oxford for an exchange program. I thought it sounded intriguing and so I applied for it and got in. After junior year I headed to Europe to travel for about six weeks before starting school. I had originally started the trip as the only girl traveling with five of my boyfriend's fraternity brothers, also ultimately headed to Oxford. Not the best plan. They treated me like one of them and there were no issues between us. But they wanted to go places and stay places that I was not completely comfortable with. I was pretty frustrated and unhappy early on. In one of the more serendipitous events of my life (and I've had several), while traveling in Switzerland, we ran into two people from Duke—a guy and a girl—whom my travel buddies knew. We talked to them for a while on the train platform. I got to know the girl, Stacey, who confided that she was unhappy with her travel companion who apparently had not "gotten the memo" that they were only friends, as she had a boyfriend back at Duke. I likewise told her I was not enjoying my trip either, and in the roughly twenty minutes that we talked, we decided to ditch the guys and strike off on our own.

Stacey and I traveled for weeks together and had one adventure after another. She was a complete joy and I can truly say, the first person I found to be a true soulmate. She also had tinges of this outsider complex. She was crazy smart and didn't always fit in socially the way she wanted to. We recognized a part of ourselves in the other. We remained close both at Oxford and back at Duke later for senior year. As a matter of fact, she is still a close friend—and my longest-lasting friend today. The fact that she ultimately became a psychiatrist is just an added perk! Yes, taking chances can have unintended consequences and downsides—it can also provide you with gifts that will surprise and delight and enrich your life. I am a true believer in the risk-reward paradigm.

The protocol for learning at Oxford is very different from the university experience in the United States. Classes are really only lectures and they are optional. They cover a variety of topics and are taught by leaders in each field. But the real work is done one-on-one with a tutor assigned to you upon arriving. I lived in New College and my tutor was in Balliol College. I had chosen British Political System as my course, and so each week my tutor would assign a paper to write on a given topic and asked that I come to a specific point of view on the question/topic. I was on my own to figure out what to read, how to research, and ways to structure my paper in order to come up with a point of view on the matter at hand. Each week, I would submit my paper and then go "defend" it while he peppered me with questions. I loved the approach. It taught me to think independently. It taught me to structure arguments in a logical fashion. I was forced to debate and defend my conclusions. This nascent skill of learning to react unemotionally and logically with facts and data proved to be immensely important for me; I called upon it time and time again in stressful or combative business situations later in life.

My time at Oxford was a real highlight and I felt more at home there than I ever had at Duke. I learned a lot along the way. I attended some amazing lectures and I traveled all over the UK. I was sad to have it end, but returned to Duke a stronger person and a better critical thinker.

All of this growth came in mighty handy when I got back to Duke, because my life imploded almost immediately. For starters, it turns out the boyfriend I thought I'd marry had been dating someone all summer, much to my surprise. He broke up with me and absolutely crushed me emotionally for most of my senior year. I felt, once again, disconnected to my friends, similar to when I went back to high school for graduation. Most of my friends were his friends and I realized that I had molded much of my existence around him—his friends, his interests, his view of the future. I was modeling my mother's behavior toward my father. But this was no "savior" whom I'd known since seventh grade. This was a twenty-year-old boy who was growing up and sowing his oats, at my expense. I learned a life lesson about finding my own voice—but it would take years for that to develop.

During my senior year at Duke, I was completely lost, likely clinically depressed, and struggling to find a path to graduation. I stopped the party scene. I hung out with my friends from Oxford instead of my old friends. I focused on looking at law schools; I took the GMAT as a warm-up before I signed up to take the LSAT. I was stunned when the results came back—I hit the ball out of the park and had a really high score in my back pocket. Still, I was unmotivated and barely making it through my classes and my waitressing shifts. After graduation I stayed in Durham and picked up more shifts at the restaurant.

The summer ticked by but my mood never improved. My roommates were worried about me. My family was worried about me. Eventually, sometime around Labor Day I think, my father called and essentially told me to get my act together and figure something out. He said he had not paid the exorbitant tuition money for me to be a waitress in Durham, North Carolina. So my roommates and I opened a bottle of wine, got out a map of the US, and talked about where I should go. New York, to my mind, was out of the question because I would have to live at home in that boring, comfortable suburban house with my parents and take a train into the city each day—a two-hour commute, minimum. *No thanks.* LA was too far to drive. But Chicago? I could drive to Chicago. I knew one or two people (literally) there but it was a start.

With even the discussion of it, I started to feel my old juices flowing again after almost a year of misery. I started to get excited. The only problem was, I had no money, no job, and no idea how to start. But isn't that how every hero's journey begins? Until you feel completely lost, you won't find the courage to take bold action—courage is borne of necessity. But it can launch you into a wild adventure! I drove home to New Jersey and asked my father if I could borrow $2,000 to move to Chicago and look for a job. Miraculously, he agreed. I will never understand why he did that; he was a conservative man and this was a crazy, half-baked idea. But I think the depression that he'd observed and the new energy in my voice must have hit his soft spot. He probably would have agreed to almost anything to get me up on my feet again.

With a used car I had bought postgraduation, $2,000, and a back seat holding literally all of my stuff, I drove to Chicago. I checked into a small room in a boarding house in Evanston, Illinois, and rented a typewriter. I sent out letters to all five of the top banks in Chicago asking if they had had any cancellations in their commercial lending training programs. I figured I would at least start to see a bit about business through a bank, which would lead to all kinds of different companies. I had absolutely no idea what I was doing. I'd never tracked down my friends in Chicago, so I was on my own. But I felt alive again and I was both energized by the adventure and stressed by the $2,000 I now owed my father.

It turned out to be a lesson in trusting the universe. Four out of the five banks replied that they had cancellations and invited me to interview. I had multiple job offers within six weeks of getting to Chicago. I never would have had this level of success had I interviewed on campus in the traditional approach to finding a job. I looked at acceptance rates for various programs today—not yesteryear which I am referring to here—but it was still interesting. Oxford University has a 17.5 percent acceptance rate; Harvard is 3.2 percent. A Navy Seal has a 1.5 percent chance of being accepted. But Goldman Sachs?

Goldman has a 0.33 percent acceptance rate. Now, I did not apply to Goldman Sachs and commercial banking is not as competitive, today or yesteryear, but it does give you a sense for the fact that these training programs are very popular and very competitive. The fact that I had multiple job offers to join just before the program started is the ultimate lesson in the potential benefits of not trying to plan things, especially at this stage of life. So I accepted a job in the cash management training program at a major Chicago bank, and I started in October. I had a real job, and found myself a tiny studio apartment in the gold coast of Chicago. I owned a sofa bed, a small coffee table, and a secondhand desk. I knew no one. I was on my way.

Outward Bound

At one of the firms where I worked, the Big Boss decided that we as an executive team needed to bond more—build relationships, learn to trust each other…you get the drift. So he hired an outside group to come in and take us on some "outdoor adventures." These were usually over a weekend, so in addition to the forced "enjoyment" of the great outdoors with nine of your favorite coworkers (including the CEO, your boss), you had to figure out what to do with your children for that time period. There was, shall we say, both involuntary physical and involuntary financial investment.

I was the only woman on the executive team, so there were a few logistical issues from the get-go. When we had to change clothes, where did I go? Did I have separate sleeping quarters? My own bathroom? Remember, these were not hotels—this was the great outdoors! And so began a most uncomfortable series of adventures—all involving an overnight trip and a series of problem-solving exercises. It usually involved the group of us having to put our heads together to figure out how to overcome an obstacle. At the end of the evening there was time in either a swimming pool or a hot tub, to grab a drink and "unwind." Since these involved bathing suits, a lot of the time it made me very uncomfortable.

I can't say that any of my coworkers were anything other than sympathetic to my plight; they were polite and respectful and worried for me at the constant awkwardness and discomfort. Yet, because most of the tasks assigned required figuring out how to do something to someone, it was invariably me that became the vessel that everything was enacted upon. I got sent down a river, lifted to a high tree branch, balanced on shoulders, and carried through the woods. There is one cringey photograph from this time that shows me being hoisted over a wall—you only see my ass and nine guys' hands on it pushing me over! (And they posted that in the cafeteria as a sign of senior leadership unity!)

After a series of these outward bound trips, I decided I'd had enough and it was time to speak up. I went to the CEO and explained that although the program was designed to take all of us out of our comfort zones, I thought it was disproportionately "uncomfortable" to me. He listened and offered a suggestion—"Why don't you design the next one and come up with an exercise that you think is fairer."

I thought about it, and came up with a simple, inexpensive, un-woodsy idea that would be easy for all of us to do—even in the office. We would give each other manicures! How hard could that be? Any gal knows that the easy chitchat that happens at a nail salon creates a pleasant bond between both the practitioner and the recipient.

I pitched the idea to my boss and he promptly decided the program had fulfilled its goal. There was no need to do any more. Program canceled.

And—from my point of view—**mission accomplished!**

2

Learning to Compete

"Don't be distracted by criticism. Remember—the only taste of success some people have is when they take a bite out of you."

—Anonymous

Up until and through college, if you come from an upper-middle-class background like me, your whole life is scripted. The major decisions and next steps are laid out. Sure—where you go to college and what you major in can be choices, but they are choices within a very confined decision set. Once you graduate, and even in the months leading up to graduation, all of a sudden there is no script. Not only that, but for some odd reason the "world" (defined as every adult ahead of you in life and in your sphere) expects you to not only have a plan but know *exactly* how that plan will unfold. For me—and I assume for a lot of people—this produced a sort of *Alice in Wonderland* anxiety. Yes, I had dutifully followed the expected course and secured a first job. Yes, I did not live in my parents' basement. But I had no idea what a nine-to-five job was even like—much less whether I'd picked the right one for me.

The chances of your first job being a perfect—or even a good—fit are pretty slim. What unfolded for me and what those first few years taught me, if nothing else, is that adulting is hard. Without the protection of any "expected" guardrails and lacking solid self-knowledge or -awareness, I became immediately and intimately acquainted with my new friend "impostor syndrome." While attending my training sessions, dutifully taking notes, introducing myself time and time again, and participating when I could in meetings, I carried around with me (in addition to my ugly, masculine briefcase) a pile of self-doubt and fear. The constant, nagging questions of "Am I good enough?" "How do I stack up?" and even "What the hell am I doing?" kept me company night and day.

Nevertheless, I cobbled together the best professional wardrobe that I could on a budget, which in those days consisted for us gals of trying to look like a man. Power suits with patterned bowties, pantyhose, and medium-heeled shoes. Nothing too sexy; nothing too casual. Nothing, in fact, that had much personality at all! It was all about fitting in. My one big splurge I remember was for a beautiful pair of leather pumps, in burgundy leather because, I figured, those would match blue, black, or brown wardrobe choices. I loved those shoes, and I assumed that they blended in to my new professional image seamlessly. Imagine how hard I chuckled then when—literally decades later—I ran into a woman who worked with me at the bank. I did not remember her but she remembered me. "Oh," she said all those years later, "you're the gal that wore the same pair of shoes every day!" *Sigh.*

But all of this reflection came much later. At that point, on October 1, I put on my big-girl pantyhose and took the bus downtown to start my first real job. Now, this particular bank was at the time a well-respected bank founded in the Midwest, and traditionally *the* bank for the aristocratic families of that part of the country. A lot has changed since, and they, like other banks, have had to adjust to the times. But when I worked there, it still had that panache of old money and solid tradition. What I remember about my start there was that it was a very quiet and restrained atmosphere. The dress code was formal. There was an open floor concept with bankers working at their desks, and only the department manager had an office. There was a hierarchy system—if you were new like me, your desk was the first in line. Behind you was the next person in seniority, and the final desk in a three-desk column was the most experienced person. They had the privilege of sitting by the window. The reporting relationships were reflected in the desk alignment; in other words, I reported to the "desk" behind me and he reported to the "window desk." The window desk people reported directly to the department head in the corner office. And by the way, we are not talking about a big, glamorous corner office—those were many floors up. These were small, square, utilitarian corner offices.

Everything was new for me. The routine of a nine-to-five job was new. Waking up early and commuting was new. But having a pay-check was also new. My starting salary was $17,500. It didn't take me long to realize that I had some pretty stringent budget restraints, especially if I was saving to pay my father back. I quickly determined that having a roommate would allow me some financial flexibility and also afford me a larger space.

My tiny, cramped studio apartment was already feeling stifling to me. Since I was meeting a lot of folks my age in the training program, I soon found a great roommate and she and I took over the lease from some more-senior trainees at the bank who were moving out. I soon learned that it was who you knew that could change your fortunes, whether it was finding a great apartment or getting fixed up on a date. The clubby atmosphere fostered a sense of belonging, and a group of us hung out often after work and on the weekends. Most of the people were Midwestern—Chicago being the big-city draw for grads of Illinois, Michigan, Indiana, and the like. The Midwestern friendliness was a huge boost to me while I navigated a completely new city and its surroundings. I felt very grown-up while I rode the 151 bus from the gold coast to the financial district and met friends for cocktails after work. It was a heady time.

The work itself was pretty dry and I barely used anything that I had learned in college. I was in a training program that assigned me to the various cash management products for three months each: correspondent banking, lockbox services, treasure services, and some smaller areas. Each three-month stint allowed me to meet new people and have some limited client interaction. The correspondent bank training had me taking my very first business trips, which were to smaller Midwestern cities to sell our services to smaller regional banks. The best part of that was seeing so much of the country I had had no exposure to before: Birmingham, Kansas City, St. Louis, Memphis, and the like. I found the smaller town bankers to be salt-of-the earth types who knew their customers so well they could discuss their children's names and home addresses by heart. I often reflected on this later in my career when I was surrounded by narcissistic powermongers who had no time or interest for anyone else. It was refreshing ... yet boring.

At the conclusion of my first year, two important things happened. First, the cash management team was relegated to a new location in a building across the street. At first, we felt offended, as we were clearly the ones who weren't important enough to be in the main bank. But it turned out to unleash a much-improved atmosphere. The stuffiness was gone and the team became more animated and lively. People talked more, joked around, and weren't as tied to their desks. It became more fun.

Second, my fellow trainees and I took our "test" to see if we passed the program and could be permanently assigned to a group. This was a sort of oral exam, where we would present the products and answer questions from an assembled group of senior bankers. We had to present as a group—so you didn't exactly know which part you would be expected to cover. For me, this seemed slightly nerve-racking but essentially no worse than what I'd had to do at Oxford. But for others it was terrifying, almost paralyzing. I was surprised and concerned when I saw how poorly some performed and how intimidated they were. Some froze. Some couldn't answer questions. Not everyone made it. But I passed and I was assigned to one of the product teams. I liked my boss, I liked my colleagues, and I liked the enhanced client contact and travel. I did not, however, find the work any less boring. But I did have a few experiences that built my confidence, and as is so often the case, they were trial by fire.

One happened when my boss had a conflict and couldn't handle both an important meeting with an existing client and a business development meeting with a potential new client. He was forced to send me alone to the pitch meeting. It was with a large office supply company which today has about $8 billion in revenue. I was fresh out of training and had never handled any meeting alone before. I don't remember much about that meeting—but we won the business. And I remember the somewhat surprised look on my boss's face when he got the news. That was a feeling I'd never forget and I discovered there can be a fun side to being underestimated!

The other was when I was invited to have lunch with some other newbies with some of the bank's senior management in the executive dining room up on the top floor. I am sure they did this with many younger associates—but it seemed not every single younger or newer person got the invite. It gave me a boost, for sure. And decades later, serendipitously, I was invited to a dinner for women in the Chicago area who sit on public company boards. It was hosted at that bank in the very same executive dining room. Although the people and circumstances were quite different, it was hard not to reflect on what a long journey it had been and how much I had accomplished from that very early start. I remembered when I was young, riding up in that elevator, feeling anxious and uncomfortable. This time, when the doors opened there were all kinds of people there to greet us and "escort" us into the dining room. The contrast was stark.

Years even after that, someone asked me in an interview when I truly felt like I had "made it." And that moment of walking back into that dining room in a much more revered setting is exactly what came to mind. And I remember the interviewer was surprised. She reminded me of some other successes—more public and known—and asked me if maybe those could have been "the moment." But no; for me it was a memory having to do with an early invitation—promising hope and a small amount of encouragement, leading decades later to a private sense of victory—that meant the most.

Still, in the back of my mind throughout the two years or so that I was at the bank, I kept thinking about graduate school. I had never found the time to take the LSAT. In addition, my work at the bank exposed me to a contract-review process that we were required to master as part of our training. When I struggled to read paragraph-long sentences and confusing clauses starting with "wherein" and "hereto," I quickly decided that law was dry and boring. (This is years before I worked with outstanding attorneys in more varied fields than banking law . . . mergers and acquisitions [M&A] and litigation have to be some of the most challenging and dynamic careers out there. I just didn't appreciate that at the time.) So I started focusing on business schools. After all, I still had that great GMAT score and writing the applications didn't seem that daunting. But I could never actually pull the trigger.

While my work life was stagnant, my social life was really happy for the first time since college. I also had a new boyfriend. I always thought that if I went to business school it would be Wharton, and I just wasn't ready to relocate from Chicago. An incident changed that perspective, however, which also left a lifelong scar in my adjustment to the business world. I took my first vacation! That may not seem traumatic, but it turned out to be.

I don't remember where I even went on this vacation or anything that transpired during my trip. What is burned into my brain is arriving for my first day back. I rode the elevator up to my area and found … nothing! All of the desks were gone and the space was completely empty. I was stunned, confused, and scared. What had happened? Did I have a job? I was told to "go talk to HR." I didn't even know anyone in HR. I found my way to their floor, asked to speak to someone, and then waited.

What seemed like an eternity later, a mid-level executive invited me into her office and informed me that the cash management team had been restructured and was now not only located on a different floor, but was half the size that it had been (one week ago!), and that yes, I had a job but no, it wasn't my old job. I had been moved into a new area. I was very shaken by this and astounded that no one thought to tell me; either before I left, or had a plan to connect with me upon returning. I naively blamed the bank as an entity and swore to never work for such an insensitive place again. (Ha!—just wait.) I dutifully showed up for my new role but completed the business school applications that weekend. In their callous treatment of me, they lost me. It was a lesson I retained for life. And to this day, whenever I'm returning from vacations, I always breathe a sigh of relief when things are exactly the same as before I left.

* * *

Grad school applications took some of my focus away from the smarting that I felt at the "redistribution" of my job duties. It was the first time in my life that I merely "phoned it in" at work; it would not be the last. I applied to a handful of schools—Wharton still being my top choice. I don't remember exactly where I applied, but the results were good. The only school I remember getting rejected from was Yale. My research was obviously pretty bad because after I received the rejection letter, I looked into it and learned that Yale had a significant nonprofit bent to its studies. As I recall, my essay was all about my passion for being a striving capitalist. No wonder they didn't see me as a match! But the "capitalist" essay seemed to work with my other top choices, and after receiving acceptances from several (including Wharton and the University of Chicago), I accepted Wharton.

This is where life gets in the way sometimes and what you think might be a linear path takes a sudden turn. It all started with a fire.

My boyfriend and I had been dating for several months at the time. I was living in my beautiful apartment with my roommate and my life had settled into a nice, early-stage adulting lifestyle. I was happy—outside of the boring job that had dislocated me. One Saturday night, just before the time that the job change happened, the three of us—my roommate, my boyfriend, and I—were playing a board game in the living room of my apartment. Suddenly, all three of us noticed that the apartment felt hot. Imagine our shock when we opened the door to the kitchen and the entire small room was engulfed in flames! We called 9-1-1 and quickly alerted our landlord and our neighbors and prepared to evacuate the building. The fire department came and put out the fire but the apartment was a mess. Smoke and water damage had infiltrated every square inch of the apartment and the kitchen was gutted. We were quite shaken—being in our early twenties, none of us had any experience with anything like this.

My roommate went to her parents' house in the suburbs and I stayed with a friend. Given that it had occurred on a weekend, we had a little time to get parental advice and think through our next steps. This entailed contacting a lawyer and learning about our rights. On Monday, we discovered that our landlord was accusing us of starting the fire and claimed that because it had occurred in the kitchen, we must have been cooking (we weren't) and that grease was the cause of the fire. Clearly this was going to get ugly. We responded (through our new lawyer) that we were in no way responsible and that the apartment was now uninhabitable and therefore we would be terminating our lease and moving out. This dispute went on for some time and caused great distress for both of us (along with our parents). The eventual resolution was in our favor because the fire department had categorized the cause of the fire as electrical. So we were off the hook (except for the lawyer's fees we had to find a way to pay).

The fire changed everything—and I mean *everything*. I needed a place to live. Quickly. My roommate decided to live at home for an indefinite period after that to save some money. I didn't have that choice. So my boyfriend and I decided to move in together. We had been dating for a while and it seemed to be a logical next step. We weren't thinking much beyond that at this point. We found a small apartment right around the corner from where I had been living and moved in shortly after the fire. It all happened very quickly and very unexpectedly. It was from this new apartment that I completed my grad school applications. Several months later, when the acceptances came in and I decided to go to Wharton, my boyfriend and I hit a little minicrisis. He was not happy at my choice of Wharton. I thought we could do a long-distance relationship but he balked at that idea. Suddenly, I had a huge choice to make.

I had always viewed Chicago as a short-term stop—always assuming I would return to the East Coast to settle. Chicago was a "spread your wings" kind of phase for me and I wanted to prove to myself that I could conquer the basics of self-sufficiency ... finding a job, creating a life postcollege, and recovering from my senior year setback. Wharton fit the bill perfectly in terms of my "plan": I could return to the East Coast, I liked Philadelphia a lot (my father had graduated from vet school at Penn), and I still had college connections around that area to kick-start a social life. I had not yet taken the time to take stock of the investment I had made in creating this new Chicago life. But it was time to.

Once my boyfriend asked me to reconsider, I had a difficult decision on my hands. I still felt a pull to the East Coast and I was proud and excited that I had gotten into Wharton. But I was happy in Chicago and the two years I had invested there had provided good friends, a happy relationship, and a vibrant city life. I did not know

Philadelphia very well, I realized. I did know New York and it did not appeal to me as a long-term answer. Chicago had all of the cultural advantages of New York, but it was cleaner, smaller, more livable. OK, the winters were terrible—but Philly and New York didn't offer much better in that regard. The University of Chicago was a top school and, I figured, a heavy-hitting finance school that could really add a serious credential to my résumé. How serious was I about this guy? How important was where I went to grad school to a future career? What were my priorities?

It was a difficult decision—my parents pressured me to head to the East Coast. My father had warned me when he lent me the $2,000 that I was at an age where I could very likely get "entrenched" in the Midwest—that I was at a life stage where I would make personal and professional connections that would make it hard to leave. And his warning was prescient.... My friends wanted me to stay and I came to understand the value of the community I had created. So I decided to stay in Chicago. I called to see if the University of Chicago would allow me to reverse my decision and accept me as a full-time first-year MBA student. Once they agreed, I reversed my acceptance of Wharton. I "picked" my relationship—and although our eventual marriage ended in divorce some years later, literally everything in my life tumbled from this fork-in-the-road decision. And I have had no regrets. He was and is still a good man. I would never have had my oldest son, nor would I have had the subsequent relationships, children, and jobs that followed. I had no idea of the gravity of the decision at the time. But life has a way of doing that sometimes: You only realize things in retrospect.

In the fall of 1983, I started my studies in Hyde Park at the beautiful gothic campus of the University of Chicago. If Duke was relatively comfortable for me academically, the University of Chicago was a cold bucket of water chilling me to the bone. I have never worked harder in my life. Everything was different from Duke. The weather and the culture were both chillier. I did not feel a connection with many of my classmates. It felt ultracompetitive from the start. Now, I understood that grad school was supposed to be different: more intense, less social, deeply focused on the area of study that you were pursuing. But the intensity at U of C was unlike anything I had ever experienced.

And so I began to appreciate how loud the voice in my head could be. As if it wasn't hard enough to step up into this competitive environment, I had a daily battle of hearing a scared, overwhelmed voice inside repeatedly saying, "This is too hard," "You're not as smart as they are," "You are not special," and "What are you doing here?" Now, I am aware that a lot of people have that voice in their head and there are probably many versions of that out there related to whatever your unique life experiences have been up to that point. As a matter of fact, someone specifically asked me to include addressing the concept in this book because she struggled so much trying to silence that voice. (See Chapter 13). And I would simply say this—everyone has a voice in their head, maybe more than one. I have a duet in my head—ranging from my mother's critical take on things trending toward the "You're not so special" variety to my dad's more constructive life lessons, including "If you are going to do a job, then do it right." Some are healthier than others. But make no mistake about it—it is up to *you* and you alone to silence the demons and listen to the angels. I am not a psychologist and can't pretend to do more than make basic observations about this. From my perspective, I think it's important to do the work merely to identify whose voice it is that you are hearing. Then challenge yourself to do some digging into that to understand it better, take from it what you deem healthy, and "break up" with the rest. Write a "Dear Bad Voice in my Head" letter and exorcise it! It will do you no good in the long run.

Back to U of C—the composition of my class was predominantly male, with a heavy Asian concentration. I was in awe of the brain power that surrounded me. It was the first time (but not the last) that impostor syndrome came roaring at me. I felt slower, less sharp, less nimble on my toes than I perceived my classmates to be. To compound the issue, Duke had been largely big lecture formats with tests and papers to assess performance. Much of U of C was taught via the Socratic method, where students were randomly called on and class participation mattered in terms of peer respect and as part of the actual grades. That method was originated by Christopher Columbus Langdell in 1870, and now 97 percent of law professors (but not necessarily business professors) use it today, according to Friedland (1996) and Fullum (2015). I had a serious confidence problem and lived in fear of being called on, so you can imagine how well that went for me when it actually did happen.

I remember that one time when I was called upon, I had lost the page that we were on (OK, maybe I was daydreaming a bit)—I will never forget the beating of my heart and the panic while the professor continued to ask, "Ms. Jamison? Ms. JAMISON???" Eventually I mumbled something and he moved on. But I remember another mortifying experience for one of my classmates; it was a business law class and the case involved the Arthur Murray School of Dance and whether or not they had a fiduciary duty breach when they milked an elderly lady for thousands of dollars because they told her she had a "future" in dance. When the professor called on this poor man in my class and asked his opinion, the guy said that they likely had liability.

"Why?" the professor asked.

"Because she was a bad dancer," he answered.

"Mr. So-and-So, would you please come up to the front of the class?" Once he was up there, the professor commanded, "Now, dance." The guy started jumping around while the class roared. Obviously, the case did not turn on whether or not the lady could dance and the professor used this guy to make that point. I felt for him and I remember it to this day—talk about toughening us up!

I was paying for grad school myself. My father had generously paid for all of undergrad, but made it clear to each of his daughters that if we wanted to continue, we needed to fund it, which I respected. There were a lot of balls to juggle. I had to take out a lot of student loans to pay for school and even then, had to find part-time work to bring it all together. My old employer, the bank, offered to employ me part time. So for more than two years I went to school full time and worked part time in the evenings, taking the train from Hyde Park up to the Loop and working well into the night.

When I look back, I wonder how I did it with such a rigorous course load, not to mention the safety concerns of traveling alone back and forth at night. In addition, I found the curriculum challenging. Everything was graded on a curve in the MBA program, which meant that regardless of how well you did on a test, a certain percentage of the class would fail if they were in the bottom tier of performance. The competition was fierce. There was also a distinctively quantitative orientation to learning about business. There was a heavy emphasis on statistics and mathematical insights. There was not a lot of group work . . . it was a school for individual achievers.

Since I honestly didn't feel like I had the innate mental abilities to compete, I fell back on hard work and thorough preparation to ensure that I didn't end up on the bottom. I spent hours organizing and outlining and memorizing. I made what friends I could find with a few other women, and we supported each other. I also got married and settled into being a newlywed. So my life was somewhat multifaceted but also predominantly focused on school. I was under a lot of stress—even more than I realized at the time, and I'm sure that didn't start my married life off on the best footing. Those two years went by very slowly and I felt constantly stretched, mentally and physically, by the grind.

I was forced to grow in a lot of ways, sometimes painfully, for which I am forever grateful to U of C. I became used to competing. I learned to contribute in class with more confidence. I gained a tremendous amount of self-respect for overcoming my fears and proving to myself that I could survive in such a tough environment. Believe me, those skills came in mighty handy in later years. I learned to think analytically. I learned to juggle priorities. I learned what it was like to live with debt. I learned that difficult times do, eventually, pass. As a woman, I truly started to grasp what it was like to be part of a minority in a male-oriented environment—and you better believe the world of finance was and still is a male-oriented environment.

Let's just talk about that for a minute.

After spending decades in the business world with men and having raised four sons and married more than one man, I think I basically have a PhD in speaking "man." And I love men; I appreciate men; I have learned so much and have had rich experiences with every variety of man that exists out there, at least it feels that way. But, especially back then with Baby Boomer bosses, they often just can't help themselves. The interrupting, the talking over, and the mansplaining was incessant, insulting, and inefficient. The "surprise" when you could actually handle a crisis without crying, or make a tough call and fire someone, or stand up to intense questioning was almost comical (except that it's not). The subtle sexual tension and not-so-subtle harassment were omnipresent. It doesn't mean you can't succeed and thrive. It doesn't mean that you can't acknowledge this and still have genuine respect for these people in other ways. It doesn't even preclude becoming friends with some of them—which is actually a conduit to some "teachable moments" where maybe some growth and change can occur. *That* is what my generation put up with to make it at least a bit better today for the women who came after us. And the men of the next generation—probably raised by mothers who lived within this environment at some point who schooled them—are better.

I have come to believe that the most important muscle you can build is resilience. And like a muscle, it gets stronger with use. While it takes a lot of fortitude to go through tough times, they *are* what make you stronger. In my career I have had to face distressed business situations, ethical dilemmas, toxic environments, and mental illness emergencies (not mine!); I have had times when I was extremely concerned about reputational damage and financial ruin. In all of those cases, things eventually sorted themselves out. But there was trauma involved. The silver lining of that trauma, though, was that I grew so strong—strong enough to know that I could weather it, that "this too shall pass." One of my favorite quotes of all time is "You're never as good as you think you are, and you're never as bad as you think you are." Think about it. Embrace the trauma for the lessons it's teaching you and move forward.

On that note, most people know who Roger Federer is—one of the best tennis players of all time. He is also known for being approachable, incredibly graceful, and, obviously, ferociously competitive. Roger gave the commencement address at Dartmouth in 2024. In it, he made some powerful comments about moving forward. He started by stating that over the course of his tennis career, he won roughly 80 percent of his matches. But then he quoted an interesting statistic. How many points had he won? he asked. The answer—about 54 percent. So even with such smashing (pun intended) success, he only won a little more than half of the actual points.

So he said, in a sport like that where you lose almost half of the points (and that is as a top-ranked player!)—you *have* to learn "not to dwell."

"When it's behind you," he says, "it leaves you fresh to commit to the next point."

He then said, "*When* you lose, and you *will* lose, it is natural to doubt yourself, and to feel sorry for yourself. But your opponent has self-doubt too—never forget that. Negative energy is wasted energy. So here is what you do: You accept it, you cry it out if you need to, you force a smile, and you move on."

Adapt and grow, he counsels. Work harder and work smarter. Go forward—learn not to dwell. Accept that you may lose half of the time. It doesn't mean you can't ultimately win!

Bad Day

In the nineties Hillary Clinton wore headbands, which I thought was a pretty cool look. So for a period of time, I integrated them into my wardrobe. I also, at that time, tended to bring a glass of wine with me to sip while I read before bed.

After work one night I came home, changed my clothes, and headed downstairs to cook dinner. My kids were playing around the house and my husband was talking to me while I cooked. I heard some small footsteps and turned around to see my middle son—in first grade at the time—walking into the kitchen wearing the following: my bra (hanging on top of his T-shirt), the hairband I had had on earlier in the day, and an empty wine glass that he held in his hand as if he were chatting at a cocktail party. And, while I stared at him, he said, "I had such a shitty day!"

My husband looked at him, looked at me, and said, "Bingo!!"

I decided then and there to watch my mouth and try to be a little less grumpy when I came home from work.

3

A Graduation Surprise

"The only thing a person can ever really do is keep moving forward. Take that big leap forward without hesitation, without once looking back. Simply forget the past and forge toward the future."

—Alyson Noel

In the middle of my second year, I started interviewing for jobs. Frankly, I didn't really have a lot of time for this and tried to be as efficient as possible. At that time, investment banking was the be-all-and-end-all for prestige jobs to secure coming out of business school. The large banks would come to campus and invite certain students to interview. While the competition was fierce, I found that getting an invitation to interview was not very hard if you were a woman. I learned that being in the minority could be both a blessing and a curse; it just depended on the circumstances.

There are times when being a diversity candidate can help you take advantage of being in the right place at the right time to open doors and foster growth; there are also times when it can eliminate you from the pool of applicants without you even knowing about the opportunity. In my career I have been excluded from the good ol' boys' club about as often as I've been considered for an opportunity strictly because I was a woman. I would say for me personally it wasn't strictly a blessing or a curse—although it was both at various times. I remember reading one of my CFO references from a man I deeply respected and worked well with for years. I had asked him to provide a reference for me for a CFO role I was vying for (and won). Years later I had a chance to read the notes from those reference calls and I was stunned to see that his first sentence was "I expected to be disappointed and I was delighted not to be. . . ." He then went on to say many positive things. But that sentence just floored me. Why did he expect to be disappointed? And who starts a good reference out like that?!?

Anyway, I attended a number of these and quickly assessed that I was not a fit for investment banking. Typically, the bank would host a large group dinner at a trendy restaurant downtown. They would send a handful of bankers to wine and dine us in the types of places we could never dream of affording—then use those dinners to determine whom they'd like to invite to a one-on-one interview. The conversations were strange, a combination of pointed and combative while they assessed us, but then very solicitous when they tried to sell us on the lifestyle and riches that awaited us if we were ultimately chosen. I thought the entire game was stupid. To me, the approach seemed pretentious and arrogant. And while they tried to make the life of an investment banker seem sexy, we all knew that they would work you eighty to a hundred hours a week in exchange for that high salary they touted. I looked around the table and thought, "These are not the kinds of people I want to work with every day." After the first few of these, I started declining the invites.

I was wondering where to look for the next career move. What type of place should I find? Where would I fit? I had no idea. And sometimes the universe steps in and something unexpected presents itself. I think you have to pay attention when that happens!

In my second year of business school, an opportunity came to me through the university. A top accounting firm was a powerhouse company in Chicago. They typically recruited in various universities at the undergrad level for starting accountant positions. However, in 1984, when I was in the second half of the two-year MBA program, they approached the graduate business school looking for two "guinea pigs" to help them launch a litigation consulting practice within a small internal unit called Special Services—outside of the traditional accounting or tax divisions that were so profitable. Somehow my name was surfaced. It is a mystery to me to this day why and how my name came up, but I was approached about being interviewed. So I did. Never turn down at least exploring an opportunity that seemingly comes out of nowhere!

Going through the interview process, I remember feeling intrigued; I had never considered public accounting as a next step. And although I had learned basic accounting in my first year of business school, I wasn't exactly an accounting whiz. But that (supposedly) didn't matter because this consulting group would work with clients engaged in meaningful commercial litigation where damage assessments, using advanced modeling and financial concepts like discounted cash flow, would determine the range of outcomes for either juries or judges to decide. It sounded like a good way to put my new skills to use in a variety of contexts. I thought I could continue to grow and learn.

The only catch was that they wanted the two of us to start in the spring because of tax and audit seasonal staffing demands that typically constrained human resources at that point in the year. I wish I had been savvy enough to ask a few more questions about this since it clearly flew in the face of their recruiting pitch, that accounting knowledge didn't matter because we would be separate. But I accepted it at face value and agreed to leave the full-time program in the spring term and finish my MBA at night so that I could grab this opportunity. This elongated my graduation by six months.

From the get-go things didn't go as planned. For starters, the first thing they asked me to do was lead an audit . . . yes, *lead* an audit. I had never even been *on* an audit! It was insane for them to think that I could come in in a leadership position on day one and lead a staff competently.

Bear in mind I had no management experience at all—at the bank, I'd never had direct reports. In addition, the client they put me on was a hospital sixty minutes outside of the city, so I had a terrible commute. The client, having no extra room to use for auditors, put us in a broom closet. I am not kidding—I was working at a portable desk in a broom closet! It was a disaster. And I was still taking night classes simultaneously to complete my MBA. The audit was completed largely because of the extra hands-on work completed by the manager above me. Whether or not he just didn't "get the memo" about me and the new position I was in, or if he was just perhaps resentful because of the extra time involved to rescue the audit in the middle of busy season, I am not sure.

This could have been a teaching moment for him to help me get up to speed, but instead, he was surly and very obviously resentful that he was working with a completely inexperienced team leader. At the end of the project, he graded me at the lowest possible rating category, which left me humiliated and confused as to how this complete mess happened. Clearly the leaders of the Special Services division hadn't thought through this new program very well. Again, it was a bad start for me. I was very passive and very stressed. The impostor syndrome sat next to me every day. How I wish back then I had had more courage to just simply advocate for myself and raise the issue. Any sane manager would think that putting me in charge of the audit was stupid. But I was determined, stupidly, to soldier on and not complain. It would be years before I finally learned that lesson.

After that, audit season thankfully ended and I joined the consulting group with my self-confidence materially diminished. I was assigned a cubicle in a small room with eight guys—a small, enclosed room. It was claustrophobic enough, but back in those days, you could still smoke at work and several of them smoked cigarettes and cigars during the day. Obviously, it was less than ideal, and I became acquainted with my local dry cleaner pretty quickly! But I was put on an interesting project—the MCI v. AT&T lawsuit, which ultimately became a Supreme Court case years later . . . but this was early stages.

MCI brought an antitrust suit against AT&T, alleging that AT&T compromised MCI's profitability because AT&T refused to provide interconnections between the two systems so that calls could be completed on the MCI network. AT&T claimed that they would not provide connection services to a direct competitor. AT&T's attorneys, Sidley Austin, hired our accounting firm to calculate damages from lost profitability to refute any calculations MCI would submit. The case lasted most of the time that I was at the accounting firm, eventually settling (only to resurface later with different issues and charges).

Although I enjoyed parts of the project, it was strange to focus only on a small portion of the larger issue. We were also to be at the beck and call of the lawyers, who seemingly changed their minds a lot and adjusted their directions to us as their defense strategy morphed over time. They also seemed to like to work at night a lot! The overall manager on the project for the firm was a brilliant, friendly guy who ran the project with ease. Unfortunately, that left him with a lot of time to party and there was pressure to go for expensive, alcohol-fueled lunches that would stretch long into the afternoons. I hated these and felt lousy (physically and mentally) about it, but it seemed to be expected to be seen as "part of the team." I was learning a lot about culture or lack thereof!

Throughout all of this I had been juggling work during the day and school at night. My husband had decided to get his MBA at night too, so he was doing night courses as well. I don't even remember how we managed to pay for all of those classes but I do remember money being really tight. We thought that once we both graduated, we'd be rolling in money and could dig ourselves out of the debt hole that we had created.

Eventually I had completed my night classes and was ready to graduate. The relief was enormous—I had been carrying both a job and school together in one shape or form for almost three years at this point, and it was exhausting. I relished the idea of only having one area of focus and assumed I could really give my all to my job. And, since the AT&T case was heading toward a settlement at that point, I looked forward to a new assignment and perhaps a team I could more comfortably be a part of.

As graduation approached, I started feeling sick a lot. I was also gaining weight, which I assumed was a result of the long, liquid lunches. I invited my parents up to attend my graduation. The ceremony was lovely, held in the cathedral on campus, and afterward we went out for a celebration dinner. On our way into the restaurant, I began to feel sick and shortly thereafter woke up on the floor with my father talking to me and rubbing my neck. I had fainted. Concerned, I made an appointment to see my doctor a few days later. She, too, was concerned. A few days after that, she called with the results of the blood work. I was about seven weeks pregnant. I had had no idea and had been religious about using birth control. I was the "1 percent" when they say that a birth control method is 99 percent effective. My husband and I were shocked. Once again, things seemed to be taking a turn I had never expected.

Eating It Up

I was traveling in New York when I needed to finish writing and then reviewing a 10-K filing, which is the financial reporting required by the SEC annually for public companies. These are a bear to write and then must go through extensive review with the auditors and lawyers. They are usually a hundred-plus pages.

I was hungry, so I went to a restaurant near my hotel where they had an open kitchen concept. I sat at the counter that faced the kitchen where you could watch them cook (if you weren't working on a 10-K!). It typically took a few hours to finalize and review these reports, so I figured I could eat while I worked.

When I first sat down the server placed some food in front of me and said, "This is to get you started." I started reading and nibbling at the food, which just kept coming for some reason! I was distracted, deep in my numbers and my narrative—so I just spaced out and never noticed the fact that I hadn't ever placed an order. Yet, the food kept coming and I kept munching away.

After a bit, they cleared the food away from the gentlemen next to me and handed him a dessert menu. He took the menu, turned to me, gently nudged me, and said, "Well, what should we get for dessert?"

Suddenly, it clicked. I had been reaching over and eating his food the entire time I had been sitting there! He never said a word—but he did look mighty amused when he asked me about dessert. I was mortified. I tripped all over myself to apologize and offered to pay for his meal. He refused. He must have been an attorney because he said he noticed I was working on a 10-K and he knew how intense that was, so he was "happy to contribute to the cause." What a great sport!

Whoever he is, I thank him—and so do my sisters who love to tell that story at parties!

4

Birthing My Future

"My entire life can be described in one sentence:
It didn't go as planned and that's OK."

—Anonymous

To say that my pregnancy was not only unexpected but quite traumatic would be an understatement. I struggled initially with the "normal" first-term issues of nausea and exhaustion, all the while trying to keep up a brave face at work. I still shared a crowded workspace with the smokers, which more than once caused me to run to the bathroom to be sick. I hadn't told work yet about the pregnancy, so I was trying hard to act normally—all the while facing numerous biological challenges. It soon became impossible.

My doctor had noticed that my blood pressure kept rising. I assumed it was because of the pressures of work and hiding my condition. I explained to her that I really believed it was driven by anxiety. Ultimately, she really didn't care what the root cause was (nor should she)—it was a danger to the fetus and we had to make it stop. The only answer was complete bed rest. The same day that I informed the accounting firm about my pregnancy I also presented them with doctor's orders for complete bed rest—and ended up on short-term disability. It seemed I had no sooner started my nascent career than it was derailed.

Now if you've read this far, you probably have learned enough about me to know that being confined with nothing to do is really not my cup of tea. I remember that one of the very first days of my confinement (as they used to say historically—now I know why!) was when the *Challenger* explosion occurred. I must have watched the replay of that dozens of times while lying in bed. With the hormones raging, I was extremely emotional about literally watching the deaths of those astronauts. In those first few weeks, I gained a lot of weight and did a lot of crossword puzzles. This was going to be interminable. I needed a project.

In those days, the internet was basic and wasn't the foundational source of all knowledge that it is today. So I turned to books. I was allowed to get up for one hour per day, and one day, I walked to a bookstore to browse. I looked through the professional section when I noticed the CPA study guide. I had never had any interest in getting a CPA, even though I worked at an accounting firm. After my first disastrous experience with auditing, I'd never planned to raise my hand to do that ever again—not that I had ever exactly raised my hand the first time! Yet, bizarrely, the four-inch-thick manual called to me because it looked like something that could engage me for the next many weeks. It was better than crossword puzzles or endless fiction novels. I bought it. Maybe it would stem my appetite too?

I settled into a routine of sorts. Morning talk shows, followed by two hours of CPA study. Then a lunch break and a brief walk. Back to the CPA study for another two hours and then maybe some letters or phone calls. It wasn't perfect but it also wasn't forever. The CPA exam was in late May and the baby was due in early June. It would be tight but it could work. My doctor was entertained somewhat by this, and at each appointment she would ask me if I was on track. She thought that since I would be essentially at term, it would be OK to get up to take the test. Time ticked by slowly, and I was mighty sick and tired of both being pregnant and doing accounting problems by late May. The blood pressure issue exacerbated fluid retention and I was quite huge; by the end of the pregnancy, I had gained eighty pounds! It was exhausting.

When it was time to take the exam, I was thrilled—but only because I was allowed out of bed for the first time in months. Under any other circumstances, I would have cursed the fact that my first days of freedom were spent taking a three-day exam, but I truly didn't mind. I was ready to be intellectually challenged, and to my mind, the exam represented the end of the purgatory and the start of the next chapter—motherhood!

I showed up for the exam and waddled back to my assigned seat. I may have imagined it, but it seemed every eyeball in the room was on me. (Of course, most of the test takers were male.) I still remember the horrified look on my seatmate's face when I dropped down next to him (hemorrhoid pillow in tow!). Fortunately, he was a dad and had been within close proximity to a pregnant woman before that day. He was actually very sweet and, at each break, made sure I was OK and brought me water. As I took that test, I remember thinking two things during the first two days: a) This test is L-O-N-G and b) If I don't pass, I am never taking it again!

On the third and final day of the test—well, you guessed it, I woke up with labor pains. The final day was only half the length of the previous two, so I was incredibly close to finishing. I couldn't give up on it now! I called my doctor's answering service and asked to talk to her, saying it was urgent. She called me back and told me she could give me something to stop the contractions. So I went to her office early in the morning, got the medicine, and finished the test. Yes, I was compulsive! Nicholas was not born for another three (endless) weeks—whatever she gave me more than did the trick. But my compulsiveness paid off . . . I passed the test.

The birth wasn't much better. My doctor, whom I was very comfortable with, had a fever and was out that day. I had one of her (male) partners whom I had never met to deliver me. And, despite getting to the hospital with plenty of time to spare, my medical team "missed" the window to give me the epidural. It seemed the maternity ward was busy that day and my contractions started out slowly but then progressed quickly—too quickly to give the epidural. I had no intention of doing natural childbirth! My entire family was in medicine and I am a firm believer in medical science. But there I was, with my (male) doctor telling me, "Don't worry—you're going quickly; it won't take long."

But after my transition period and once fully dilated, something happened—the baby got "stuck." No movement for six hours. I pushed and pushed and pushed. It was exhausting. I have never felt such pain. I think I even fainted at one point. I remember thinking I would end up with a C-section. . . . But when I told the (male) doctor that I was ready to give up, he just put his face very close to mine and said, "This baby is too far down for a C-section and too high up to use forceps. You will either push this baby out, or I'll have to saw through your pelvic bone to get it." He really did have a lousy bedside manner.

I pushed the baby out within the next few pushes—having had the fear of God put into me. But even that wasn't smooth. When we finally dislodged little Nicholas, and they wheeled me into the delivery room (the baby coming finally very fast now) there seemed to be a huge commotion. People were running down the hall, yelling for more attendants and seeming quite upset. I was obviously in no position for conversation at this point, but I was scared and confused. My medical team stayed with me, eventually put me in a room nearby, and Nicholas was born. Shortly afterward, they told me that the woman in the next room had died; she had had an aneurysm while delivering *and* she was the wife of one of the doctors in the hospital. It was tragic. Nothing about this delivery went as planned. And little Nicholas, who has today grown into a handsome man, had a bruised, misshapen head after being stuck for so long. I don't believe either one of us was much to look at by the end of that long day.

* * *

My maternity leave was the normal six weeks—so much shorter than what the norm is today—and was spent as most are: learning how to care for an infant, trying to sleep when possible, and working hard to start losing the enormous amount of weight I had gained. When I returned to the accounting firm, I felt distinctly out of place. I hadn't been there in so long, and everything about my life I had changed in the meantime. My body had been through a lot, my homelife now involved an early-morning drop-off at a babysitter's house, and I was starting the juggling act that would become my new normal for the next two decades.

But at that point it was all new. The company really didn't know what to do with me initially—it was summer and a slower period, so they seemed to struggle to find much for me to do. Remember, at this point I had virtually no real experience in banking or accounting. Some exposure, sure, but not a depth of experience that they could mine for clients. My "big business" career had gone off the rails before it could really start! The days were long and boring. Actually, they were a weird combination of boredom and stress and exhaustion all rolled up in one big ball of anxiety.

Eventually they put me on a project—I don't even remember now what it was, but what I do remember is that the partner had a tendency to wait until the very end of the day (or later) to review the work.

When I look back on that, and how different it is today with longer maternity leaves and, in some cases, the opportunity for paternity leave, I am glad that we have made progress here. But in the early eighties, things were so different and men in power positions gave no thought to the struggles that women went through. And it wasn't just parental issues—I remember struggling to make it to the dry cleaner's by six to pick up clothes. Men weren't the ones who typically had to worry about such mundane things; they had wives or housekeepers for that. But despite the improvements in some of these areas today, I personally think that the business world is still really lacking in empathy. I think it is a critical success factor in effective leadership— you simply cannot earn people's loyalty if you haven't taken the time to understand who they are or what they're up against and try to work with, not against, them.

My husband and I had bought our first house during my maternity leave. (Here's a piece of advice: It's a bad idea to move when you've just had your first baby!) Our little house was in a suburb, necessitating a train commute into the office five days a week. I would awaken early, drive the baby to the sitter, return the car to our house, and then walk to the train station. My husband would pick him up at the end of the day. Theoretically, this worked well—we were sharing the responsibility and I had some flexibility at the end of my workday, even if the mornings were quite hectic. But the train schedule was difficult past a certain time at night. If I needed to work later to meet with the partner, which happened often, I would be relegated to "local" trains that made a lot of stops and left only hourly. I was getting home late often, even though my work was done easily within the regular workday. I often didn't even see the baby at all . . . arriving home after he went to sleep.

I tried to approach the partner about the difficulty I was having, and instead of being flexible, or even just empathetic, he told me that my approaching him on this issue really made him question my commitment to the job. That was very discouraging. Honestly, I felt beholden to the accounting firm since they had supported me through my pregnancy, but I was starting to realize that the accounting world at that point was a distinctly unfamily-friendly place. And I internalized the lesson that you don't complain, you don't expect understanding, and you just have to figure it all out on your own. These guys with, for the most part, stay-at-home wives didn't have a clue.

Nick was an easy baby and we loved his babysitter. But she lived in a high-rise apartment and transporting him took some time each day. I missed a lot of time with him that first year thanks to the partner on my project, and it made me sad. I felt like everyone around me knew my baby better than I did. I also experienced my first shaming: One day in the elevator after dropping him off, a total stranger turned to me and said, "I think you should be ashamed of yourself—abandoning your child." I was speechless. It seemed so cruel and unnecessary. We could not afford to live on one salary at that point, and the truth was that my career was going better than my husband's. I needed to work. Judgment is a bitch—especially when you are struggling and insecure. It sort of worms its way into your consciousness and eats away at you, causing you to feel unsure, inexperienced, and inadequate. I wonder if people ever think about the power of their words when they randomly comment on someone else's choices?

Shortly after that, as my routine continued unabated and the partner kept up the later hours, I got my first-ever headhunter call. Talk about a much-needed ego boost! It seemed a major consumer products company was looking for a financial analyst. I jumped at the chance to interview. From the moment I started meeting the folks there, I knew I wanted that job. It seemed like a fun, high-energy place to work. It would involve a drive rather than a train commute, but I came to love that drive over the years for the small amount of quiet time it provided (at least until car phones came along). It was too good to be true; they offered me the job, a big salary increase, and even a bonus opportunity. I was really excited.

* * *

The next four years of my life were wonderful. To this day the closest friends I have made came from those years. The place was filled with super smart, fun people, and the work experience was different from anything I had experienced in my two previous jobs. In both banking and accounting, my work life had been filled with financial people all doing similar jobs—making for a competitive environment with a fairly one-dimensional view into business. Here, the brand management system meant that marketing ruled the roost, and each brand manager was tasked with managing every element of a particular business. As the financial analyst on a business, I brought only one perspective to a multifaceted discussion and decision-making process.

For the very first time I was able to hear all functional perspectives: marketing, sales, operations, legal. It was also different in that there was no "client" per se. All of the decisions revolved around increasing value through either customer perception, effective cost management, or creative ideas for new products. The culture was completely different from anywhere I had ever worked before; there were fun outings, creative sessions, food tastings. Outside of work there were informal get-togethers and a few team sports. There was laughter and creativity and casual conversation. It was fascinating and engaging. I learned so much. While I brought the financial perspective to any discussion, I realized that the "right" financial answer wasn't always the best answer for any variety of reasons. I learned to think holistically.

Those early years at the consumer products company were some of the happiest in my life. I was learning and growing; Nicholas grew into toddlerhood and then early childhood as a curious and obedient child. I had wonderful friends and felt so lucky to work at a place where the training programs were terrific and the leadership was strong. I excelled and was promoted several times within a short period of time. I came in as a financial analyst, then became a senior financial analyst, a manager, and ultimately, a director. At the time I was proud of myself for moving so quickly up the corporate ladder. Now, looking back on it, I think I was promoted too quickly and the foundational skills—particularly related to leadership and communication—were lacking. I realize now that I had a simultaneous "gift" and a "curse," in that I can be very good at "selling" myself. I give a great interview and I can talk a great game. But selling yourself into a role and doing the role competently are two very different things.

I also found myself surprised at my success in this regard and so accepted what was offered out of gratitude and pride, but without really critically evaluating either the roles or my skill sets to effectively fulfill them. Ultimately, I learned that through some very painful lessons, and my final years there dealt me that first blow. Because after surviving the first few promotions, I was finally promoted into a job that was over my head and too much of a stretch. And that combined with one of the worst bosses I've ever had, who—far from trying to help me figure it out—really came down hard on me.

A Fiery Exit

I was in Boston for a conference and had a work deadline, so I decided to grab a glass of wine at the steakhouse across the street from my hotel. I had some work to do that involved reading an SEC filing, so I printed out the voluminous pages and headed over there. The bar was dimly lit with candles on the high-top tables, where I plunked down to settle in for a while.

Everything was great—the wine was wonderful and I was plowing through my work, reading page after page, making my comments in the margins, and flipping the pages that I had finished. All of a sudden, I smelled smoke. Even more alarming, the smoke seemed dangerously close to me, truly hair-raising(!)—I realized I'd set my papers on fire when the pages I'd flipped got too close to the candle on the table.

The fire was small and easy to put out—but it was pretty obvious to all around, including the bartender, what had happened. And, while I quickly apologized to everyone around me and assured them the fire was out, it proved to be too late...you guessed it, the sprinklers came on! They had to clear the bar.

I picked up my charred papers, mumbled a hundred apologies, and quickly beat a hasty retreat from that place.

As it happens, it is still one of my favorite bars in Boston and I have been back many times. Each and every time I remember that experience and chuckle. (I also take note when there are candles on the tables and try to act very responsibly.)

5

A Taste of Toxic Leadership

"Narcissists will destroy your life, erode your self-esteem, and do it with such stealth as to make you feel that you are the one that's letting them down."

—Anonymous

LinkedIn survey by *Forbes* magazine reports that seven in ten US workers say they would quit their jobs over a bad manager. And a study by Life Meets Work found that 56 percent of American workers claim their boss is mildly or highly toxic. A *Harvard Business Review* survey reveals that 58 percent of people say they trust a stranger more than they trust their boss! The American Psychological Association found that 75 percent of Americans think their boss is "the most stressful part of their workday." To me, these statistics are not surprising at all. The toll a bad boss can take is immense and can be very scarring. Most people ascend in business because they performed in their *functional* role—but have little to no idea about managing others. And so a lot of unprepared, insecure, high-achieving performers, who do well individually, become thrust all of a sudden into management roles over others. I know because I was one of them. I had to "figure it out" and learn on the job. Mostly, I did with my people management what I'd done as a mother—veer *away* from the styles that had been modeled for me—but that still left a lot of room for error. Since I spent the majority of my management years in crisis leadership positions, the leadership style I developed had more to do with selecting the right people who could deal with the chaos of crisis, rather than the long-term career development that more stable companies provide. I think they're different skill sets.

A recent study by CareerBuilder.com shows that 58 percent of managers said they didn't receive any management training. My guess is that that is understated. There are *so* many ways to be bad at this that it is amazing there are even a small percentage of great leaders out there. Yes, it can be taught, but it so often isn't, leaving the vast majority of bosses leaning on their innate abilities (or not) to predict success. In the meantime, hundreds, thousands, even millions of us suffer, laboring under managers who don't know how to model empathy, respect, or even, in some cases, common decency. I experienced this firsthand at around thirty years old.

* * *

In my final years at the consumer products company, I had already moved between divisions and become responsible for increasing numbers of people. It was a challenge to try to learn leadership "on the job" and I'm sure I made many mistakes along the way. Although the company had those good training programs, most were oriented to technical skills or strategic thinking. I don't remember ever having a leadership class. Nor was anything like that taught in business school. You just had to figure it out on your own. I had worked for various people by that point, at the bank, the accounting firm, and then this company. Certainly, personalities varied greatly and leadership styles followed suit. Although I liked some more than others, each were either a neutral or positive presence, and I tried to learn what I could from each of them. That was about to change.

When I was promoted for the final time, I landed in a corporate planning role. At the time, an outside company had just acquired us and the culture and atmosphere changed quite quickly. Through rounds of layoffs, there was a lot of fear. And the new guys were intent on running the company like they ran their other companies, even though the products involved and the metrics for success were completely different. Very quickly my department was overrun by requests and demands that made no sense—yet had to be complied with—so we were working a lot of late nights. Due to my frequent schedule changes, I lost several nannies that year and I began to feel overwhelmed and exhausted. I remember a few times falling asleep at a red light while driving home at night. But that wasn't the real problem.

My boss, I'll call him Pete, *was* the problem. A real yes-man to the acquirers in an attempt to get in with them, he committed my team to any number of projects—usually without consulting me. He had a habit of calling me into his office to go through his to-do list, never once asking about mine. He was crass and misogynistic—once "jokingly" telling me to sleep with an outside service provider so that we could get a fee reduction. He asked one of my female managers to describe the inside of the women's locker room in our fitness center and asked whether or not the women walked around naked. And he was duplicitous: There were a number of times he would lie to me about who asked for what or why something was needed, or would only tell me part of the background so that I sounded stupid in meetings. The few times I went to him for help, he was dismissive. I remember at one point I thought my executive assistant had a drinking problem. I asked his advice and he sternly said, "We're not ever going to talk about that—you are slandering her." Once again, I felt completely on my own . . . and incessantly attacked.

And although he was the worst, he wasn't the only toxic piece of the new environment. When the new company held a worldwide finance conference that year, it included all kinds of large meetings with keynote speakers and wonderful activities—no expense was spared. The senior leadership was in attendance. At first, I enjoyed it. (Who doesn't love a good boondoggle?) But two things happened to sour it and show me what true harassment was like.

The first occurred after an outing on a boat—we had a group of about ten people and it was a lovely afternoon. The captain was a hoot and loved to play games and ask questions. As we pulled back into the dock, he asked one last question: "Who was dressed the best for the outing?" We all looked around and no one said anything. We were all wearing bathing suits. Finally, the captain himself pointed to me and said, "I'll pick her—I like her suit." That was it—it was very innocuous. But apparently someone reported it when talking about the afternoon.

Later that evening, there was a large dinner banquet and they were going to give awards for the afternoon activities—best golf score, most fish caught, etc. I was tired and sunburned, so I left the dinner and headed to bed early. In the morning, the phone rang in my hotel room and a female coworker of mine said, "Has anyone told you about last night?" I was confused. I told her I went to bed early. "Oh," she said. "I know. Everyone knows, because they called you to get the award for best costume on stage for your bathing suit. The senior executive kept talking about it and making jokes about what must have been so special about your bathing suit. He asked if it 'showed anything'—then when you weren't there to come up on stage he asked—from the stage—what room you were in and made a joke about having to 'check out' this outfit personally." I was horrified and embarrassed. Later that day several people who had been on the boat with me gave me their condolences and said it was disgusting and assured me that I had done nothing wrong.

The following night, the second piece of harassment came to light. I decided to have a glass of wine at the bar. I was not enjoying the conference at that point, because I was still humiliated and felt conspicuous about the bathing-suit episode. How unfair that I felt so bad when the perpetrator could have cared less. I wanted some time to escape with my own thoughts. Another senior executive ended up sitting next to me at the bar. He made polite conversation and asked about my job, my time at the company, and my career aspirations. I remember thinking it was a good conversation and perhaps one that would stand me in good stead while I tried to learn to work with the new guys. I excused myself to go to the bathroom and when I returned, my "new friend" said he had a present for me and slid a napkin across the space in the bar between us. I looked under the napkin and there was a condom. I politely slid it back to him and left the bar.

Things with Pete continued to go badly and I got to the point where just showing up at work every day took tremendous fortitude. It is clear to me looking back that I did not have the courage to confront the situation. If I had stood up for myself, perhaps it would have ended better. Instead, I hung on and hoped things would get better. But, as they say, hope is not a strategy. It was clear that I was not doing a good job, but his demands were also unreasonable and unfair and his emotional swings and abuse were classic narcissism. My frustration at the endless and pointless requests, coupled with the disruption at home of constantly trying to find better childcare, along with Pete's narcissistic tendencies, were all taking a great toll. And, although I didn't take the logical step of reaching out for help, or directly addressing my performance and issues with Pete, I did quietly start looking for a new job. I had had enough of finance and felt I wanted to try something different. This would turn out to be the first but not the last time that I voted myself off of the finance island.

In retrospect, I wish I hadn't let myself feel chased out. I had had a stellar career trajectory up until then and I could have traded on that with those inside who supported me and had promoted me in the past. Why I felt so isolated is a shame—and a bit of a mystery to me to this day. There are many articles and studies about working for a narcissist, including one in the *Harvard Business Review* in April 2016 by Rebecca Knight. Virtually all of them reference the isolation people feel when working for one, so I guess I wasn't alone (pun intended). But most recommend that you get yourself out of there, since "making it work" doesn't usually work.

Because I was looking to make a functional change, it took some time to identify logical next career moves that branched out. Eventually, I landed an offer from an HR consulting firm that wanted a more quantitative approach to bring to their executive compensation practice. The timing was good, because around the time that I landed that offer, I had my performance review with Pete. He gave me a terrible review—replete with comments that were both insulting and untrue. He graded me the lowest possible ranking. In delivering it, he was quite harsh. Although I knew I had issues, this was beyond anything I would have expected. There was obviously no arguing with him. I sat with it for a few days … embarrassed, shocked, and humiliated … and then went above his head to an even higher senior executive—and someone who would later become the CEO. Finally! I found some courage and had some agency!

I didn't know this person well, but I felt I needed some confirmation that my career was, in fact, in such terrible trouble. In the meeting, I told him that I was not there to argue the details of the review (which might have been stupid, in retrospect). I simply had one question for him and one question only: Did he agree and support the review? He did. He said that he was not familiar with my performance per se but that he trusted Pete's judgment. I thanked him and left. It shouldn't have surprised me that virtually no attempt was made to look into, understand, research, and come up with his own opinion . . . but it did. The good ol' boy network bands together when threatened. It took me a while to realize that powerful men tend to back each other up. I should have come to that meeting with data and details of my performance and examples of ways that Pete had not supported me. I should have come from a position of power, and not that of a victim. Perhaps if I had threatened a lawsuit or something, it might have elicited more of a response, but we shouldn't have to threaten legal action to have a fair conversation . . . and, by the way, with that comes a huge personal downside. But I learned that tough times require backbone and I should have been my own advocate sooner and better. The next day I resigned, very grateful to have the new job offer in hand.

Imagine my surprise then when all hell broke loose and that same senior executive called me in for a meeting and begged me to stay. "Why?" I asked. What had changed in twenty-four hours to make him so keen to keep me? What a shit show. These guys didn't know the first thing about real communication and leadership. He rambled on about numbers and resources and talked about transferring me if Pete was the only issue. I was very confused but also somewhat amused by the sudden turnaround. One thing was clear—I wanted out and I was not going to negotiate to stay where I had received no support. In fact, having experienced this from both sides, I do not recommend ever allowing yourself to be induced to change your mind after resigning. Yes, they may pay you more money or make other concessions. But believe me, upper management will not forget that you resigned once and you might do it again. Your loyalty will be forever in doubt. Better to make the change and get a fresh start.

The whole experience led me to think hard about what was so different here and why it was so painful. I had to compare Pete and his boss with others I had worked for in the past. A great leader knows the difference between confidence and arrogance. Someone with confidence has a strong sense of self, and they are comfortable expressing their specific point of view, but they also respect debate. They pick their battles and fight fairly. They can admit that others can be right, and when they themselves are wrong. They are no strangers to empathy, and often start sentences with "we." An arrogant leader has to be right. They compete with their staff and peers. Often, they will take on another's point of view as their own. They view the world as a battlefield, and refuse to give in. Their narcissistic tendencies are evident, and judgment is common. Rarely will they show a vulnerable side, and they start most sentences with "I." There's also a sexist element that comes into effect in many workplaces, since it's (very unfortunately) still a man's world.

Primarily, I think the most profound difference is around communication—or lack thereof. The worst bosses I've had were terrible listeners, asked few or no clarifying questions, and seemed to want to rush the conversation to a fast conclusion. That impatience makes the other person feel small and unimportant . . . which is exactly how a narcissist wants you to feel. Communication is a power play for them, not a bona fide resolution vehicle.

Forbes reports that 76 percent of high-performing women get negative feedback . . . versus 2 percent (2 percent!!) for men. I don't know a woman in my board world who hasn't faced a similar challenge, either working for a narcissist or facing sexism. As a matter of fact, most women—between 54 percent and 81 percent—report experiencing some sort of sexual harassment at work. It's a sad fact of life. But I will say this: If you are dealing with either narcissism or sexism, head for the hills. It will not get better and people like that don't change. You will be the one to pay the price!

Looking back at it, Pete could have taken a much different approach with me—had we both just acknowledged that I was in over my head, we could have either worked out a solution or he could have mentored me to help me get on my feet. But he had no interest in helping me; he was purely self-promoting. When I had my exit interview with HR, I gave the example of going to him for help regarding my executive assistant and my concern with her drinking. The HR person, who had no idea what Pete had said to me, told me that Pete had come to her for advice because he had noticed the same thing. She said she told him that privacy issues were paramount and that he should be very careful in discussing this issue with anyone. How ironic—and so maddening!—Pete had not only seen what I saw but also reached out for help. Instead of shutting me down so abruptly, he could have shared that experience and we could have had a much more constructive conversation.

I was more than ready to move on. But the lessons that Pete taught me lasted. Working for a narcissist is hard—but putting your head in the sand and hoping it will get better is not an effective strategy. I should have tried harder to communicate with him, and failing that, I should have gone both to his higher-ups and to HR sooner. I probably could have effected a better solution so that I would not have felt so powerless and essentially run out of the company. It took many years to look back on the experience more objectively—not only to admit that I had been in over my head, but also to have grace with myself and realize that I was dealt a rough hand. And I believe in karma. Pete had a meteoric career after that—until he didn't. He was "involuntarily fired for cause" by a later employer, the facts about which are quite murky. But when that happened, years later, I received a call from the lawyers asking for a character reference on Pete. Boy, was I happy to provide one.

I wish I could say that Pete was the only bad boss in my career, but there would be more. And with those challenges came even more hard-earned lessons.

Special Payroll

In one of my CFO jobs, I was heading out on vacation just before the quarter end, when sales commissions were paid. I needed to authorize the special payroll run, and understandably, a lot of people cared a lot about whether or not it was processed in a timely manner.

There were some mechanical issues earlier in the day which delayed my ability to approve it before I left the office and headed to the airport. I got the "all clear" from the vendor just as I was getting to the airport, so I quickly approved the payments.

In my haste, I decided to just do a company-wide email to alert everyone that the problem was fixed and the funds were deposited. I titled this email "Special Payroll," hit send, and boarded my flight.

Well—so much for quality control. My autocorrect changed the word I had misspelled (some version of "special") to "sexual."

And so, upon landing I learned that I had sent an email to the entire company titled "Sexual Payroll." Boy, oh boy, did I have hundreds of responses—mostly guffawing at my misstep, some adding a few "thoughts," others asking what I put in the payroll besides money ... you get the drift.

It was really funny and I learned that of all of the functional areas to botch something like that with—the sales people were the most responsive, the most creative, and the most merciless.

6

New Roles, New Rules

"One can choose to go back toward safety or forward toward growth. Growth must be chosen again and again; fear must be overcome again and again."

—Abraham Maslow

It took me some time to heal from the trauma that Pete and my exit from the consumer products company had caused. But, after my senior year in college, I had learned a bit about emotional recovery. This time I could not just retreat and sink into depression (although I'm sure I had a touch of it—or maybe it was just exhaustion). I needed a paycheck and I had a son to raise. It was a good opportunity to learn about "on the job" healing, which is frankly what most of us need to do while juggling the pressures of supporting ourselves.

Fortunately, I liked my new company and the approach was quite different and welcome. They were listed as one of the top 100 family-friendly workplaces, and I felt that difference.

The management was reasonable; people worked "normal" hours, outside of specific client demands. And I slowly became acclimated, learned a lot about executive compensation, and became healthier both mentally and physically. I had the time to work out; I had evenings with Nick. I came to appreciate what "balance" actually meant, and living it provided great insight into the benefits of prioritizing health, friends, and family, along with doing a good job. I stayed at that job for about three years and had my second and third sons—taking full advantage of that "family-friendly" approach!

But it wasn't only about the hours and the reduced pressure; I had two of the best bosses while I was working there. They were sane in their demands and expectations (even if the clients weren't always), and they both laid out carefully thought-through plans to execute against. They were terrific at training and mentoring and gave plenty of chances for a junior person to "shine" in a meeting—followed by thoughtful and diplomatic coaching. It is amazing how much bolder and more confident one can feel when the environment is perceived to be safe and nurturing. That was a leadership lesson I took with me for the rest of my career. Even though my later jobs were chaotic and stressful turnarounds, within each and every conversation I ever had with someone who reported to me, I tried to remember to make them feel safe and valued.

These guys also took the time to get to know each of us as individuals, celebrating my children's births and hosting their teams at their homes. Their children's pictures and awards were proudly displayed and they set the example for work expectations by taking vacations, leaving on time, and limiting the after-hours requests.

It also had an unintended benefit that makes me look back today and think there was some greater divine purpose at work for me. I ended up providing quantitative skills that they hadn't had on their team before. And the timing was perfect, since this was when more sophisticated executive compensation long-term incentive plans began to be much more complex. Stock options had been the norm, but now we had equity plans with various metrics, vesting and performance periods, and the Black–Scholes model for pricing equity variants, including stock options. This became much more commonly used as a pricing mechanism. I was often asked to build models for various clients—some of them Fortune 100—showing the array of predicted outcomes for various equity plans at differing stock appreciation levels. The senior partners often asked me to come with them to the board presentations so that if detail questions arose—which didn't happen often—I would be there to answer them. I found myself at around thirty years old, in a variety of boardrooms observing dozens of meetings. I was like a sponge—watching and learning while these very senior executives debated compensation strategy. I watched the interplay between management and board members and observed the healthy and unhealthy ways that people interacted with each other in the boardroom. And I pretty quickly observed that even though the atmosphere was vaunted, the behavior was still classically "human." Given that I ended up joining boards later, this was a great education and primer for the future. And it demystified the boardroom for me.

Over time, although I liked so much about that company, I found that consulting—and consulting on one fairly narrow topic—was starting to bore me. I wasn't looking for a job, but when the CEO of a client company approached me to consider moving to his company in a strategic planning role, I thought considering it made sense. This in and of itself was humorous because he and I did not get off to a great start.

The company was a new client and fairly small at the time, although it was publicly listed. My generous bosses, having taken me with them to much larger clients, decided that I could go solo on this one to see if I could perform well and then grow the business for the firm. The only problem was I was about seven months pregnant when this occurred. The company was located in Boston and so I flew out there for the first meeting. I will never forget the look on his face when my new client saw me, looked at my belly, and then blurted out something like "Oh, great" very sarcastically. I knew I had a lot to prove. But that's OK. Many times in business you'll need to overcome a bad start or a wonky first impression. The determination and persistence it takes to do that is a skill worth developing. In this case I worked to understand his concerns and needs, came up with an array of solid solutions, and advocated for him to individual board members. In the end, the fact that I went to bat for him in the boardroom, selling an equity plan that was fair and, since the stock appreciated handsomely, made him millions, unsurprisingly impressed him. He liked me after that!

I took the job. It would be my first vice president role; it would move me out of the HR consulting world and into corporate strategy—something I had always had an interest in and that was listed as one of my strengths in performance reviews (even Pete's). I liked the CEO and thought I could learn a lot from him (I did). It involved a relocation to Boston, but I thought I could handle that. I did not appreciate the amount of dislocation that it would cause my family—my husband had to find a new job and the kids had to make major changes—which they did not welcome. They don't really remember it now, but they had to leave the life they knew behind, start school in a new city, and make new friends. We had to get a new nanny and she had some adjustment issues as well. It was a lot to take on. It destabilized us.

In retrospect, it was naive and selfish of me to jump at this without thinking about the impact on others. And I learned a good lesson about evaluating opportunities—particularly those that involve great change—more carefully. This was a bit of an impulse decision. And while "no plan *is* the plan," that doesn't mean that every opportunity is an automatic yes. Sometimes pausing to reflect makes sense. But I didn't.

Even with the personal challenges, the good news is that I loved that job; it was a small public company, and the CEO included me in everything. I was essentially his right-hand man. My learning curve was steep but so intellectually engaging, and it was one of those roles that stands out in my mind as fundamentally changing me as an executive. I learned leadership from him, I learned influencing skills across my peer group, and I learned the intricacies of being a public company. And so it goes—now my job was great but my homelife was becoming a struggle. It is a never-ending kaleidoscope of things to balance when you are trying to juggle so many priorities.

About a year into the role, the CFO left the company and I was asked to become the interim CFO. I thought it was temporary and I really didn't want to be a CFO again—yet as time went on and the CEO didn't find a replacement he liked, I essentially played the role for the remainder of my time with that company. And it turns out, it wasn't very long. My boss had a personal situation arise which devastated his family, and his wife wanted to leave the area and move the company to a different state. He decided to relocate the company—and I decided to look for a job. Here again is an "expect the unexpected" moment. His family trauma, which had nothing whatsoever to do with that company, caused my career to take an unanticipated turn. These are the moments that those young grad students couldn't fathom when I'd asked them about being prepared for the unexpected. But they really do happen! Sure, it all worked out. But you never know when you'll be surprised. Anyway, I did not want to move again after seeing my family's adjustment issues.

And so, when an executive recruiter called (they called me more frequently now) about a financial role with a consumer products company located in the same city, it seemed like a good move to make. It would keep the family stable and it would allow me to continue employment uninterrupted. At this point, my husband's career was far less stable than mine and I was the primary breadwinner. This had occurred slowly but steadily over time. And as my husband's job changed and we moved, I didn't even realize how that shift was happening. But I felt the pressure when I paid the bills each month, and I faced the challenges of trying to juggle it all while my paycheck became the dominant and then the only paycheck, and somehow most of the child-related issues seemed to fall on me as well. I didn't have the luxury to do an extended job search. I had expensive daycare and a mortgage to pay and so I thought it made sense to take the path of least resistance and explore this new job. The only downside was that it was another financial role. While I had loved my strategy role, it was harder to find those and my résumé was stronger functionally for finance. It seemed that the executive compensation consulting and the strategic planning roles were going to be my last gasp at doing anything other than finance. I had boomeranged right back to where I had been at the consumer products company, albeit at a higher level.

From the get-go, I was bored in my new role. The company was much larger, my role was much smaller, and the culture was more formal. I was no longer invited to the wide variety of meetings I was now used to attending. The company was very successful, so my finance job was mostly planning and analysis—usually trying to figure out how to spend all of the money we were making. When I had been hired, it was as the CFO's successor. He was a Brit and originally had plans to return to the UK in one to two years' time. He was a great guy with a quirky sense of humor—he had a Spice Girls poster in his office! I enjoyed him . . . but he, unfortunately, enjoyed his job. So much so that it became apparent that he wanted to stay in the US much longer. It seemed like the road to promotion and therefore a more interesting role was going to take a long time.

And while this culture wasn't terrible, it was very different from the entrepreneurial atmosphere I was coming from. And that change impacted how I felt in the new role immediately. It never ceases to amaze me how much culture matters and how unaware many companies are—at the C-suite level anyway—of what exactly their employees find the culture to be. Bad culture is hard to define, but as they say with pornography, you'll know it when you see it. It doesn't have to reach the point of toxicity to be a less-than-ideal culture. But believe me, it is hard and slow to change. And it matters mightily.

Today, through social media, there are easy ways to learn about the culture of any company. Check out Glassdoor, for instance, to see what employees are posting about working at any particular place. Senior managers ignore this at their peril! A toxic culture can cause 20 percent of American workers to leave their jobs. It leads to a 37 percent increase in absenteeism. *MITSloan* published an article titled "Why Every Leader Needs to Worry About Toxic Culture" in March 2022, which discussed the side effects of a toxic work culture.

This was also the time when my marriage seemed to really falter. We had been under great stress since the move and he was not enjoying the impact it had had on his career, nor the geography where we were now living. We tried counseling but it really didn't offer much help. Neither one of us had good conflict-resolution skills and the exhaustion of it all caught up with us. There had been too many changes, relocations, sleepless nights, and financial pressures to allow us to enjoy life, or each other. We decided to divorce, although neither one of us was particularly happy about it. In our last joint decision, we decided that if we were going to raise our kids separately, we both would rather do it in Chicago, where he had family and I had friends.

I started a job search with the full support of my boss and who actually helped me quite a bit. Ultimately, this coincided with my first nonturnaround, noninterim CFO job offer—back in Chicago. That fell together nicely but there were ugly elements to figure out— namely, a financial settlement that set me back dramatically. Moving back was not joyful—it was practical. And the next phase of my life involved juggling being a CFO with being a single parent.

Meet My CFO

My CEO and I arrived at a law firm to participate in a mediation session to settle a lawsuit. The details escape me, but it was a suit where we were owed some money that was very meaningful to us and to the survival of the struggling company.

We were the first to arrive and we were escorted into a generic conference room to wait for the other side to appear. We took off our coats and settled in. They were late. After a few minutes I left to use the restroom. When I returned, the other side was just walking toward the door of the conference room. Thinking I would get out of their way, I scuttled in just ahead of them.

Their group—all men—very casually and very cavalierly, each handed me their coats, assuming I was the receptionist.

I collected the coats, proceeded to dump them on a chair at the end of the table, and watched their confused faces while my boss said, "Gentlemen, meet my CFO!"

7

Being a Momager

"I am not a single mom, I am a superhero in disguise."

—Anonymous

Routinely when anyone hears the term *single mom*, they respond by saying something kind and sympathetic, like "That must be so hard" or "I don't know how you did it." That's all very nice, but do many people for whom this is a theoretical ever *really* stop to think about why it is so hard? Let me tell you—it not only takes a village, it takes fortitude, resilience, energy, perspective, a sense of humor, *and* (for me) a lot of wine.

Few people go into parenthood expecting or aspiring to be a single parent, and maybe that is the first point I want to make—the prequel to what you see may be some kind of disappointment and hardship. And there are many kinds of single parents: I know married people who are, in essence, single parents. I know women who, facing their biological clock, opted to give birth and prioritize having a child over continuing to look for a mate. And I know grandparents who suddenly found themselves raising their children's children for all kinds of reasons. Personally, I think the most devastating circumstance for single parenthood is when the spouse unexpectedly exits—through death or abandonment. I can't imagine the scars and disillusionment that must come along with that. We all know that life just happens sometimes, but not having any agency at all and being handed a decades-long responsibility that you never wanted to do alone must be terrifying.

That is not my story. I made a choice for a variety of reasons—largely having less to do with my children's fathers and more to do with my belief that, for me personally, being alone was healthier and easier than being in a marriage that wasn't right for me. In fairness, my marriages were not abusive, destructive, or toxic. They were good men and they are and always were good fathers. I have no beef with them and actually love and appreciate them greatly, because I never could have done it without their participation, commitment, and constructive coparenting. My point here is not to get into my early marriages and why they didn't work—it is to honor the men I had children with and thank them for accepting my decision to go it alone. It couldn't have been easy.

Single-parenthood is less uncommon than it used to be decades ago, when divorces were much harder to get. (For example, American women did not have guaranteed equal access to credit cards or bank accounts without a man cosigning prior to 1974.) According to the US Census Bureau, as of 2024, one in four children under the age of eighteen—a total of over 17.9 million—live in a one-parent household. I played a part in finding myself raising children as a single mom—even if, even for me, there was an underlying sadness and disappointment as a result. Between that role and my intense jobs, it made for—shall we say—not quite a delicate balancing act. Instead, it was a cacophony of loud and opposing forces that slammed against each other, requiring continual and sometimes instantaneous prioritizing. I'm sure it made my life look like a comedic circus from the outside. From the inside, although certainly challenging, the experience created the most important bonds of my life, and my boys and I grew, survived, and then thrived as our small family unit found its way.

Let me start by paying tribute to my boys. I like to say I had three-and-a-half kids because my stepson came into the picture along the way and has been with me since high school. Now in his forties, he had a complicated childhood with divorced parents and was a latchkey kid through most of his early years. He is ambitious and scrappy and takes nothing for granted. He is grateful for every single gift and kindness that comes his way and is an incredibly hard worker. He has an eternally optimistic take on life. He is a survivor. My oldest biological son (the child of the CPA exam!) is a highly principled ex-military JAG, still in the reserves, and currently "involuntarily redeployed" overseas giving service to our country. He is mission and service oriented and has one of the strongest ethical compasses of anyone I know. He has high aspirations to go into public service and really wants to give back to society. My middle son is one of the most uniquely intelligent people I know, who sees connections few others see and can write beautifully to describe a point of view. He is critical, incisive, and can be a worthy opponent (and he sure was in high school!). Yet he is also bighearted and kind and emotionally expressive. My youngest is the life of the party—social and fun—but he is also incredibly hardworking and focused. He is naturally gifted with a shrewd business brain and is likely to go far. He also works his ass off. A natural leader, he gains people's respect and trust very easily.

All of them are funny; we had (and still have) so much laughter between us, which is a true gift. All are genuinely good people who are sensitive to others' priorities and feelings. They are all smart, hardworking, and unspoiled. They turned into good humans who like each other. There were times when they were growing up that I would have bet heavily against any of that coming to fruition. And as wonderful as they all are and all turned out to be—they were idiots plenty of times and learned the lessons that all of us have to through living the consequences of their less-than-stellar decisions.

There were phases:

The toddler years—boys are indestructible, which doesn't at all mean that they themselves are not destructive. Little boys are drawn to testing things through sheer physical force. Every appliance in my house had to be replaced at least once. And a lot of what they "tested" was each other. They simply couldn't keep their hands off of each other in a constant battle for dominance (or shotgun).

The awkward years—middle school is hardest on girls, but it is no picnic for boys either. This is where personality and proclivity are revealed and social status is determined—sometimes cruelly, sometimes through playground fights, and sometimes through tests and athletic tryouts that are either triumph or tragedy. Throughout, there are a lot of feelings to grapple with.

The teenage years—feelings are no longer talked about (at least not with Mom) and rebellion and boundary pushing is the day-to-day norm. Not fun for anyone involved. And so much more complicated stuff to deal with! Girlfriends, driving, friend groups, college tests and applications.

College—a new freedom for all! But financial pressures abound and "visiting" home sets up a new set of challenges where past protocols are rewired and parenting is a part-time gig.

Through it all I got very lucky in some critical ways. My kids, for one thing, were unbelievably healthy. I can count on one hand the number of times I had a work issue because one of my kids was sick. Their fathers also stepped up and played their roles, coparenting to their highest and best ability and taking the pressure off of me plenty of times. Also, I had the means to send them to great schools where the other parents and kids were good people who worked as a community for the greater good of the kids.

So my story is not a tragedy—it is a triumph! My relationship with my boys is vibrant and healthy and full of respect on all sides. With that said, let's get into the details. What exactly makes single-parenthood so hard?

First, the incessant nature of it. Every day, every decision is on you. You are the mediator in all fights; you set the rules and make the exceptions to those rules. You decide everyone's schedule every day, and you shop for and pack the food that goes along with it. You set bedtimes and boundaries and bath times and homework times and play times. You say yes to what you will buy for them and no to what you cannot or will not afford for them. You dish out hugs and punishments. Kisses and curfews. You approve (or not) of friends and field trips. You start out when the first one of them opens their eyes in the morning and you don't quit until the last one is asleep—except you don't really quit at all, because that is when you do laundry, or pack lunches, or get back online to do some work.

Next, the financial pressure is all on you—even if you have an ex who is dutifully helping. You make the decisions of how much to spend and where it goes. And the decisions can be tough. One year that I was unemployed (see Chapter 11), I took out a second mortgage on my house to pay the kids' tuitions. And it was crystal clear to me that I could only do that once before harder decisions would have to be made if my employment situation didn't improve.

And of course there is the loneliness factor. Without a trusted partner, there is no one to share the load with psychologically. No one to bounce ideas off of, to debate with, or to seek counsel from. Sure, you can (and do) ask your friends for advice—but everyone has their own parenting style and no one really knows your kids as well as you know your own. And all parents know that each and every child is different—responds and reacts uniquely—and it takes time to really talk their language. Long after the kids are in bed, there are plenty of sleepless nights where you ask yourself, "Am I doing the right thing?"

Coparenting with an ex—even the best of exes—is a unique challenge that is only exacerbated when one of you remarries and there is a new stepparent involved. Sometimes it can feel as if the "team" of parents is so busy debating and arguing amongst themselves that the children actually get lost in the shuffle. It takes a master's degree level of emotional intelligence (EQ) to effectively navigate postmarital coparenting disagreements and differing points of view. And even if ultimately fully functioning adults can get to a mutually agreeable approach—it takes energy and stamina to work through the process.

Discipline is on you—at least while the kids are in your house. You are good cop and bad cop—there's no one else to play off against. And boys are really good at pushing back, acting out, conveniently "forgetting" the deal that they struck with you, and testing the boundaries of curfews and house rules.

I do remember telling my boys in high school that they were never to drink and drive—or to get in a car with a drunk driver. I told them that whenever or wherever they were in that situation to call me and I would come get them. So one day, in the late afternoon, my middle son called me and asked me for a ride home because he didn't feel like taking public transportation. I couldn't do it, I told him, because I promised to do a favor for a friend that afternoon. He called back five minutes later: "I'm drunk," he said. "Now will you come get me?" Obviously, he was kidding—but sometimes they will find all kinds of ways to point out the flaws in your program!

The hardest and most frustrating aspect of single-parenthood is the childcare dilemma. Do you send them to daycare, which is expensive and where there is a 6:00 p.m. (sharp!) pickup time? Do you suck it up and pay a fortune for a nanny who lives with you—or nearby—and has flexibility . . . but limits the vacations you can take because of the financial drain? Do you bring an au pair over from a foreign country and *hope* that she fits and you like her? Is there an after-school program at their school? Can you count on a friend? The options go on and on—all complex, confusing, and never actually a perfect solution, no matter what you pick.

Lastly, I think one of the hardest things about being a single parent is that for years and years, there is no "thank you," no validation, no reward. It is a 24/7 job with no audience to applaud you. My friend Marc once told me that he bought a massage for a single mom in his apartment building because she looked so tired. I thought that was one of the kindest, most remarkable things I had ever heard of—that level of unexpected and generous gift is not the norm, believe me! Most of the time you are slogging it through and hoping what you're doing is good enough, while the rest of the world carries blithely on with their own lives. Self-doubt abounds.

It *is* hard. It is also a master class in multitasking, communication, boundary setting, and risk/reward analytics. (And in the teenage years there's even a little game theory involved!) Let's rachet up the support for empathy around the single moms and all that they carry on their shoulders. The business world should admire and reward their battle-proven skill set more often. Sure, they may have a few time constraints and competing priorities, but they also know how to work incredibly efficiently, juggle dozens of competing priorities, *and* they will never forget that you gave them the chance—you will have a very loyal employee!

Recipe for Success

Mornings in my house while I was a single mom were chaos unleashed. My boys have vastly different personalities and different body clocks. Two are true morning people, one is definitely not, and the fourth is somewhere in between. The not-so-morning guy was always the biggest challenge and frequently the reason for all of us to be running late.

One early morning, in the midst of alarms going off, uniform snafus, grabbing lunches, and car logistics (the morning cry of "Shotgun!!" reverberating through the house and arguments shortly following)—my son said to me, "Mom, I'm supposed to bring a recipe to school today." Well, two kids were already in the car waiting and we were running too far behind schedule for a lengthy conversation.

I thought quickly and opened the pantry, grabbed a box of Jello, and ripped the side of the box off. Problem solved! And, just as soon as that problem was raised, it was fixed, brushed aside, and quickly forgotten about … replaced by a thousand other small, sticky parenting issues to be dealt with between that morning and the end of the school year.

Imagine my surprise, then, when end-of-the-school-year-wrap-up festivities took place several months later, the teachers proudly distributed the **School Cookbook of Favorite Family Recipes** to the entire school of grades one through eight. And therein was included, along with many other recipes for my son's class, "Jamison's Jello Dessert."

8

Battle Scars

"If you are completely exhausted and don't know how you are going to keep giving this much of yourself day after day, you're probably a parent."

—Anonymous

I am very grateful for the many advances that have been made in the business world to try to help with the overused phrase "work-life balance" and fairness . . . including DEI initiatives and social-issue engagement. But I do find it somewhat comical. What life are we balancing? It makes it sound as if we are on a tightrope, at risk of falling off on the side of "work" or falling off on the other side of "life." What happens when you fall? Do you crash to the ground and die?

In reality, everyone has a multifaceted life in which choices and priorities have to be decided every day. Businesses finally woke up (to some degree) and realized that happier people make happier employees. I am not sure why that took so long, but COVID sure accelerated it. In my time, women felt immense pressure to never talk about their kids—much less their dog, their hobbies, or their eldercare issues.

But now, through the miracle of Zoom, Teams, and several years of living with your kitchen or bedroom as a backdrop, we are all much more in each other's lives. Folks join calls in all states of attitude and undress. Some of it is progress; some of it is pretty revealing. But the curtain has been pulled back and I am amused and happy to see men and women on calls holding their kids, conversing with their kids, even yelling at their kids (sometimes it's hard to remember to hit the mute button)! Life and work swirl together more than ever before. Yet, the challenges continue. Work-from-home is slowly being pressured by the erosion of workplace culture, and leadership in this time of change is tricky business. Many jobs simply can't be done from home—the hospitality industry will always require hands-on attention—no way around it. The list of the many ways that being a single parent is hard is *not* simply swept away because you can do part of your job via Zoom.

Parents today still struggle—and, if anything, some of the generational preferences and approaches have made this even harder. Kids today seem to me to be overscheduled and overprotected. I don't see a lot of downtime where they learn to entertain themselves, or navigate sibling disputes themselves. And parents are almost leaning back the other way so that children are prioritized over many other areas of life. I am not sure if this is good for the kids or not. Time will tell. But many of the young adults I see who have been raised this way aren't equipped to survive on their own yet.

My cousin leads HR for a midsized company in a traditionally male industry. She has worked hard to bring some diversity into this company and has had some success. Recently, at a business dinner she told me about, two of the young women sat by themselves at the end of a long table and talked amongst themselves throughout the meal. She approached them afterward and asked if the following night they would separate and sit with the men, because it would be a good way of integrating the group. In the morning, when she arrived in the hotel lobby, those two younger women were waiting for her. "We talked to our moms last night," they said, "and they told us that you had no right to tell us where to sit at a business dinner."

Well, I can't do anything about generational choices and parenting styles. But I can draw some conclusions and share some stories from the chaotic decades I spent as a single parent. Looking back at it with the benefit of hindsight—and knowing that all of my kids turned out to be decent people—there are a few pieces of advice I could give to those now living the life of raising a kid alone ... or even really anyone trying to walk that work-life tightrope.

Lesson #1: It is critically important to find and **build a community**. It helps with the pressures and doubts but it also helps with the day-to-day logistics. Moms "get" other moms. Reach out and start building some bridges. You will never regret it and you may just make some lifelong friends.

Lesson #2: Keep perspective and **pick your battles**—this is especially important in the teenage years. You must remember that it is their *job* to separate in those years—so let them separate. Give them some wins and some choices. Do you really care if their hair is long? Or if they aren't looking at the colleges you want them to? In my opinion, focus on the teachable choices—where lessons or ethics are involved. Where they learn about sacrifice or work ethic or meaningful consequences . . . and let the rest go.

Lesson #3: **Choose a parenting style**—and stick to it. You will notice as your kids grow that there is a wide range of styles for parenting—some are strict, some are lenient, some have looser rules, some tolerate experimentation with alcohol or marijuana. It runs the gamut. A lot of different styles can work and work well; a lot depends on who and how your kids are. But what can be disruptive and counterproductive is either not having a style (i.e., trying to be "friends" with your kid) or changing your style depending on who you are around. Peer pressure in high school exists for the parents too! Kids need consistency—and no, they won't like it or you all the time and that's OK.

Lesson #4: It's normal and natural to have plenty of doubts about parenting challenges and how to handle them . . . but ***don't* litigate things with or through your children**. It is not their job to help you parent them. And it is certainly not their job to mediate between divorced parents who haven't worked their own shit out enough to interact productively.

Lesson #5: **Outsource what you can**—and frankly what you don't care about. My daughter-in-law got this advice and I thought it was easy and effective. Is cooking dinner your favorite time of the day to talk to your kids? Keep it—but get some help for the shopping, or the school pickups or the laundry. Don't try to do it all yourself—and if you can't afford the help, then barter your way to getting help with the community that you have. One mom can do the pickups—another can do the shopping. There are all sorts of creative ways to destress your life. Don't be too proud to go there.

You can adopt these five lessons and still be very free to make your own parenting style, whatever you want it to be. Try different things in the early years, and remember that each kid is different. My biggest pet peeve is the judgment I see some parents take about other parents' parenting (or results). Be careful with that. Just because you had one obedient, people-pleasing, organized child doesn't mean you couldn't have a mini hostile dictator the next time around—or that might be the kid your friend has to reckon with, whom you judge so harshly. Bottom line: Do your best, forgive yourself, and stay out of other people's business!

I remember a therapist I once knew telling me that how you parent or the specifics of your situation is far less important than *just being there*. Constancy and love are deeply entwined. Each of my kids had their unique issues and I'm quite sure I didn't handle all of them perfectly. But I do believe that the advice I had from that therapist helped me to prioritize them when they needed it, and to show up for them, even if in the wrong way sometimes.

But I have also observed plenty of parents who overfunction for their children. Who actively solve their problems and do their homework. In one case, I know a parent who wrote her daughter's college application essays! In my opinion, that is *not* parenting; it is pandering. I wonder what that teaches a child. The people I knew who adopted this approach—whether by coincidence or not (but I think not), have children who are unemployed, are living at home, or have substance abuse issues. There is something to be said—and believe me, I know it is hard—for letting your children struggle and fail, aspire and lose, attempt and get rebuffed. I never did team sports—it's not my personality, since I liked individual activities better. But I watched what my boys learned from coaches and teams where there was a real meritocracy, but also support and guidance. It made me wish I had had more of that when I was younger. There is a reason good coaches garner such respect—they care, but they don't overfunction. They push but they don't humiliate. They teach teamwork and respect. They love winning, but they insist that the players do the work to earn the win.

I went to Duke, where basketball reigns supreme. We had a legendary coach (Coach K) who excelled at developing great players—and people—who had lifelong respect for him. Even famous NBA players looked up to him; he coached the US Olympic team to win three consecutive gold medals. And Coach K used his teaching and leadership skills to do so: "The thing I loved the most—and still love the most about teaching—is that you connect with an individual or group, and see that individual or group exceed their limits."

Leadership, coaching, and parenting all overlap. So many different faces come into our kids' lives and can have a lasting impact. And you won't really know until they are young adults who those people turn out to be for your kids, and what the lessons they took from them are. A lot of it comes down to just doing your best, crossing your fingers, and taking one day at a time.

Carpooling

One of my CFO roles had me temporarily commuting to Australia. That's right—commuting to Australia. It didn't last long, but for several months my boss and I did just that. He had agreed to take over as CEO of a company based in Adelaide, but he planned to move the company out of Australia and into the Midwestern United States. He had resigned from his previous CEO role based on the West Coast and planned to relocate his family—along with the company—within a few months.

Having just retired from my role at the CFO firm, I was looking forward to my next chapter when he called. I had worked for him previously and we had a great working relationship. He asked if I could help him for "a few months" while he transitioned everything. I agreed. But very quickly we encountered unexpected issues with moving the company internationally. We found for a period of time we had to manage the operations from afar.

We worked on a three-week rotation: He would fly over and work from Adelaide one week, I would go the following week, and we would let the on-site management handle it for the third week. I would fly over on a Saturday night, arriving on Monday morning after crossing the international date line. Adelaide is part of one of the only two time zones that use a thirty-minute mark—so from the Midwest to Adelaide, there was a twelve-and-a-half-hour time difference. Day was night, and summer was winter. It was a very **Alice in Wonderland** feeling of incongruity. I would work Monday through Thursday and then fly home all day Friday—reversing time and landing in time to be home for dinner Friday night.

I felt bad leaving my kids for a week at a time, and so I tried valiantly to make it up to them and to the other carpool moms when I returned. Working remotely offered flexibility I had not previously had, so I could offer to take on a few extra carpool duties in the weeks I was home to even things out. The problem was my exhaustion level started to build over several weeks of this crazy schedule.

One bright, sunny, warm afternoon I showed up in the carpool line and waited for the school bell to signal dismissal. Once it rang, the kids would start to come out and slowly the carpool line would move forward as kids were placed into their assigned cars. It usually took about thirty minutes. The car was warm, the music was softly playing, and I am not sure exactly when I fell asleep, but I sure did. I was out.

Apparently, cars were honking and then pulling around me to complete their pickups. I awoke to a guard pounding on the window essentially asking me, "WTF?" I sheepishly collected my kids and completed the mission ... oy.

9

Help Wanted

"A child can teach an adult three things: to be happy for no reason, to always be busy with something, and to know how to demand with all his might that which he desires."

—Paulo Coelho

These lessons didn't come easy and they aren't a panacea for everything. Believe me, I made plenty of mistakes and had some harrowing times! Being a mom is so emotional and the love is so deep that it is sometimes hard to think clearly and act rationally.

When Nick was six years old, another mother in our carpool picked up the kids on the wrong day—and so my babysitter was also at the school to pick them up. He never saw my babysitter, but got in the other mother's car and she dropped him at my house . . . but she didn't wait to make sure he got inside. She drove off! He pounded on the door and when there was no answer, he walked up and down the street crying "help me" to strangers. A kind woman found him and insisted on walking him back to my house and waited until my (completely frantic) babysitter arrived back. Unfortunately, in her own stress, she started screaming at the poor woman who walked him home. I still think to this day it is the angriest I have ever been at any human being. I called her and could not contain my expletive-filled review of her actions. I am not proud of that—and

Nick still remembers it clearly. But I learned how viscerally momma bears can react when their child is put in danger.

The topic of childcare in our society is a fraught one. According to Sonya Michel of Maryland University:

> Because of its long history and current structure, the American child care system is divided along class lines, making it difficult for parents to unite and lobby for improved services and increased public funding for child care for all children. When it comes to public provisions, the United States compares poorly with other advanced industrialized nations such as France, Sweden, and Denmark, which not only offer free or subsidized care for children over three but also provide paid maternity or parental leaves. Unlike the United States, these countries use child care not as a lever in a harsh mandatory employment policy toward low-income mothers, [but as a means of helping parents of all classes] to reconcile the demands of work and family life.

Well, I tried a number of different options in the beginning. I thought initially daycare would be fine, but the rigid hours with penalty payments for every minute that you're late eventually drove me to look for other options. I also got spooked when one of the workers at the daycare center became unusually attached to one of my sons. She offered to take him home with her if I needed extra help. Something about that creeped me out, so I turned it down. She was later terminated for "undisclosed reasons." I wanted to have more control after that about who was around my kids.

We working moms have to find something that works to handle the childcare issues that come up—especially before kindergarten. For me, that eventually turned into hiring nannies so that I could have the maximum flexibility and I felt my children were getting enough individual attention. It was the most expensive option. But I wasn't alone in selecting this. According to Zippia, there are 169,633 nannies in the US currently. Even though 93.1 percent of them are female, the women still make less than the 6.9 percent male nannies—the women make $0.97 for each $1.00 the male nanny earns.

The average nanny age is 37 years old (which surprises me, since most of mine were much younger) and the average salary is $40,262. That is after tax for the mom who pays it. That is a hefty amount to pay; it is also not enough to live on—rendering nannies a very transient job with high levels of turnover. The adjustment period for all involved is long; the reward may be short-lived. And lord, are there crazy things that can happen in your home when you have a nanny!!

One of my nannies started dating a guy while she was living with me. She was a great nanny and kept her private life separate and was fully on duty when she was supposed to be. So how did she not know her new boyfriend was an ex-con? And that guy got ahold of my debit card and started racking up bank withdrawals all over town across one afternoon, to the tune of several thousand dollars! By the time we found out, he was long gone and the money was irretrievable. Not only was her heart broken, she had to work for weeks for free to "work off" her debt to me. (She had handed him the debit card and the PIN.)

Another nanny—a nineteen-year-old college kid who was supposed to be a summer nanny for me—met the best friend of my next-door neighbor at a backyard BBQ and quit to marry the guy (in his forties) after one month. I still wonder how that marriage worked out.

Another seemed fine while she was living with us, but when she left and I was cleaning out her room, I found a collection of my sharp carving knives under her mattress!

One of my best-ever nannies was a beautiful Polish girl named Natalie. She was great at everything, except driving. She had something like five or six fender-benders while she worked for me (in my car). But she was strikingly pretty and I remember my middle son telling me, "No offense, Mom—but sometimes when you're not here, I tell people she's my mom."

One of my nannies caused a grease fire that burned down my entire kitchen—thank God she got the kids out of the house before she called 9-1-1. (I was at a business dinner.)

And then there was another terrific Polish nanny—Theresa—when I had only my oldest son. She was with him from about one year old on and was truly a second mom to him. Theresa worked in America to send monetary support back to her family in Poland; she went without seeing them for several years. She received a call in the middle of the night when Nick was about three years old and was told that her son in Poland needed an emergency operation. She left the next day, and who could blame her. She had made many sacrifices (as a lot of nannies do for their families), and of course she should be with her son at that point. Nick cried and cried and cried—and no one could ever replace her. That one was heartbreaking to watch play out. And you wonder about the long-term effects of the comings and goings of so many people in their lives.

Being a nanny is a tough job. They need to provide love, lessons, and entertainment for children who are not theirs. They do it under the watchful eye of a mother who might feel guilty, or be protective, or expect too much. They live in a house that is not theirs, drive a car they don't own, and work hours that can change often. As any stay-at-home mom can tell you, being full time with kids—especially multiple kids—takes creativity, patience, organization, and stamina. They give up a lot, and make relatively little money to do that.

It is also a challenge for the mom—who comes home from work tired and still has to face dinner, homework, bathtime, and bedtime. I remember coming into my home so many times when the nanny— understandably ready to end her shift—would hand me a verbal list of to-dos (so-and-so needs new sneakers, so-and-so has to bring a class snack to school tomorrow, so-and-so has to be at an eight a.m. tryout on Saturday) . . . you get the drift.

However you slice it, it has its challenges. The mom-nanny relationship is a weird one—they are usually young and so you become a semiparental figure to them. But they are also your employee, so it's important to establish rules and boundaries. You are also at their mercy and in their debt because they are spending so many hours with your kids and they hold their safety literally in their hands. It is an odd chemistry—especially when you share a house. Do they eat dinner with you as a family? Do they have an area in the house where they can have some privacy? Will the kids naturally gravitate to find and play with the nanny after hours—even if you'd prefer they spend that time with you? Can they bring a date home? Can they use the car in off-hours? What if they need medical attention or have some sort of emergency—then you are stuck on childcare duty, plus you need to help the nanny. There are so many things that could happen and so many things to figure out.

But discipline is probably the diciest topic. Will they discipline your children? Should they and, if so, how? Will you respect their teaching methods or will you undermine them in front of the kids, trying to be the "nice mom"? It's sometimes hard to watch the interactions between the nanny and the children, and the temptation to interfere looms large.

And of course you never know when you will walk through the door and they will give notice. Argh . . . now what? Work doesn't wait while you search for a new nanny. Even really good agencies need at least a week to find someone for you.

Yet, with all of that I still found the outside-of-the-home solutions to be harder, for me anyway, with a job that sometimes required long hours or travel. And I wanted the kids to be in their home as much as possible—the school day is long enough and is tiring for them.

But I will admit, with all of the great nannies and helpers that I had through the years, I breathed a huge sigh of relief when finally, *finally*, the boys were old enough and high school was all-encompassing enough that I didn't need full-time help anymore. Things became simpler, my semi-adults could transport themselves, handle their own schedules, and be in the house alone safely. What a huge chapter to come to a close. And, suddenly it seemed, those days were over and the specter of them actually leaving home and going to college started to loom large.

The point is: When you raise kids and you embark on bringing that village into your daily existence, it adds a layer of complexity and complication that you can't possibly understand until you're in the midst of it. The emotions it deepens, the skills it teaches, and the resilience you will find in yourself is life-changing. I have often noted, somewhat wryly, that being a single mom of boys made me a better executive, and being an executive made me a better mother of boys. I mean, saying no to a CEO is a cakewalk compared to saying no to a teenager!

Dinner Party

When my youngest went off to college, I worried for months in advance that I would be devastated. We had lived alone together for three years, since his next older brother had headed off to school. In fact, I thought I got off easy when it actually occurred.

The drop-off went smoothly; he seemed really excited and happy with his choice, and since his school was nearby, I was able to drive over to Duke and stay for a night, reliving my own college years. The weather was beautiful; my oldest son left me a memorable voicemail thanking me on behalf of all four of them for the sacrifices and for providing a great education for each of them. It was a real "moment" of feeling good. My daughter-in-law thoughtfully invited me to join her family on the Cape for a few days instead of going straight home to an empty house. Those five days were fun and I was busy and distracted.

It all went so well—until it all caught up with me.

I raised my boys in a townhouse that was attached on either side to the neighbors—in the back the balconies connected. And during my first few days home I was enjoying the peace and solitude; I was relishing in the fact that the scissors, as well as every other item in my house, were actually where they were supposed to be and I could easily put my hands on anything. I could play the music I wanted! I didn't have to wait up for teenagers anymore.

But while I was cooking dinner one night and I was sipping (too much) red wine, my youngest son's favorite playlist came on my Spotify shuffle. The first song was Lynyrd Skynyrd's "Tuesday's Gone." Oh—it got me. It got me good.

Suddenly, I remembered all of the fun things my son and I had shared— the car rides to school, the sports victories, the family vacations—and I started to cry. Not a quiet, pretty crying. Thanks to the wine, it was a full-throttled wailing! I took my glass of wine and walked out onto the balcony—still crying, trying to get some gulps of fresh air to calm down.

For whatever reason, at some point I turned my head to the left. And there were six people, forks paused midair while taking a bite, staring at me, looking quite concerned. My next-door neighbors were having a dinner party! It was so mortifying!

I gave them a very shaky smile, shrugged my shoulders, and quickly headed back inside. Very shortly after, my neighbors called to see if I was OK. So very nice of them! Still . . . so embarrassing.

10

Take This Job and . . .

"People don't leave jobs, they leave toxic work cultures."

—Dr. Amina Aitsi-Selmi

My first CFO role was a nightmare. The fact that it coincided with a divorce didn't help matters. The company was a small public company in foodservice. Recently a new investor had come in, injected some much-needed cash into the business, and relocated the company from the West Coast to Chicago. With that move came the need for an entirely new management team. I was part of this new team, as was the CEO, I'll call him Tim . . . a first-time CFO reporting to a first-time CEO. Not good. Our combined lack of experience in our roles did not blend well. And let me tell you—when there is that dynamic the CEO usually wins the day, by leaning heavily on, and blaming, his management team for failures that ultimately are driven by bad leadership. Tim was far worse than Pete—and I was more experienced now to recognize it.

My first day on the job, which was a Friday, I knew I was in for trouble. More than ten years had passed since I'd dealt with Bad Boss #1, but I still had scar tissue! I had a 103-degree fever, but showed up for work anyway—figuring I would just gut it out for part of the day to fill out the paperwork and go home.

"You look like shit," he said when I went into his office to talk with him.

"Yeah," I said sheepishly, "terrible luck to get sick right now, but I'm sure I'll be a hundred percent after the weekend."

Instead of saying something like, "Go home, feel better," he said—and I'll never forget this—"You're not gonna be one of those losers who calls in sick all the time are you? I won't deal with that. . . ."

So began the worst ten months of my life. I hated my job, I hated my divorce, and I hated Tim. Every day was a barrage of insults—not just to me but to anyone and everyone. He was outrightly abusive—at one point calling me "Helen Keller" because he said I was deaf, dumb, and blind . . . this in a meeting with other people. He made fun of people with weight problems. He taunted people for their stupidity and "dumb" ideas. It was very clear to all that he was in over his head but he, of course, would never admit that—it was all our faults. We were not working hard enough, smart enough, scrappy enough.

The fact that the business was struggling and the new investor was not happy just added to the pressure. And as a public company, the quarterly expectations from shareholders drove a short-term approach to making the numbers. The board was composed of some heavy hitters in Chicago, but they seemed removed from the details of the business and Tim was happy to keep them in the dark. We were in trouble but instead of being a team, it was every man for himself. Bad business results are stressful but can also be a great learning experience. Later on in my career as a turnaround CFO, I had wonderful experiences with terrific people, and as a team, we managed to save a lot of struggling companies. But with bad leadership it is virtually impossible to overcome the odds and this was the case here.

As Tim floundered, he became more and more abusive. He created a sense of fear in every single person who worked there and people commiserated about that quite a bit. We went through multiple rounds of layoffs. Our bank refused a loan that I had told him was unlikely from the get-go, but when it was formally denied, he blamed me in front of the board.

This was also the era of the Y2K uncertainty, when all companies feared that at the stroke of midnight on January 1, 2000, the computer systems would all shut down. I had put together a proposal to prepare us for the changeover to ensure our data was protected by updating all of the POS systems. I reviewed it with Tim in great detail ahead of requesting approval from the board. But when I presented it to the board, they balked at the price tag involved. Instead of backing me up, Tim lied outright and looked around the boardroom table and said, with a straight face, "I have never seen these numbers before and of course I would never have agreed to any of this."

Over the same ten months I was trying to conclude my divorce. The children and I were living in a tiny coach house and I could barely afford my babysitter—not to mention the support my husband was getting while we finalized things. The financial pressure was immense. Recently, while I was discussing this book with my oldest son, he shared a memory with me from this time that floored me (pun intended). I don't have any memory of it, but he said that he and his brothers were playing on the living room floor one night when I came home from that job, dressed in formal business clothes. Apparently, I walked in the door, laid down on the floor next to them in full business attire, put my head in my hands, and said, "I hate my job." That makes me sad that I felt that lost and that my kids had to see that. I'm sure it was disturbing.

On the court date, I took a half day off. Tim begrudged me this and said that if my personal life was a problem, it shouldn't impinge on work time. [Note: Several years later Tim's wife filed for divorce, and I heard that he didn't show up at work for three weeks because he was "too upset."]

The last straw for me came when Tim suggested I look at ways to change the way we recognized revenue. Not only was there clearly no alternative to our revenue recognition policy, given the kind of business we were in, but the mere fact that he would suggest it, along with suggestions to bribe contractors and other unethical proposals, led me to conclude that I had no option but to resign. This was the single scariest thing I have ever done. And this is one of many instances when the courage to do the right thing becomes paramount above all other considerations. And there were many other considerations: I had just lost more than half of my puny net worth, I was the sole financial support of my children, and my first and only CFO job had been a complete disaster. In fact, when I resigned Tim said he would make sure I never worked in Chicago again. A prophecy, I'm happy to say, that never came true. And as an aside ... who says that kind of thing? It was like a bad mafia movie!

But was it terrifying? Yes. The uncertainty and the sense of complete failure was devastating. And I felt totally alone. I was embarrassed and afraid. I did not have impostor syndrome ... I *was* an impostor. Clearly, I was a terrible CFO and I would have to find a completely different career path forward.

Because of the ethical concerns I had, and the fact that the company was public, I thought the right thing to do as I exited was to alert the chair of the audit committee as to what I had seen and witnessed. No one gave me nor even offered me an exit interview, but I felt that the shareholder's representatives (i.e., the board) should be aware that there were issues. I called the audit committee chair. She refused to take the meeting! She said that she trusted Tim completely and that she had no interest in anything I had to say because it was obviously "sour grapes." Wow—this was shades of Pete and his boss all over again, backing each other up and not playing the respective check-and-balance roles that they were supposed to play. And once again, I should have been much more forceful and required her to listen to me—or else elevated it to the chairman of the board. As an audit chair today, I have had experiences where someone in senior management requests a private conversation. I cannot in a million years imagine refusing to hear what they have to say. But that was her choice, not mine.

Sometimes, when you are so beleaguered and ignored, it's hard to find the motivation to try to save others from themselves. So I left—and I was unemployed for about a year. During that time, while I watched from afar, the company's auditors resigned, another CFO resigned, and a controller resigned ... all before the board finally woke up and fired Tim. In the end, professionally I was proven right and emerged completely unscathed reputationally. If anything, over time it actually bolstered my résumé and my reputation. But that took a long time and was never certain. The courage to act doesn't always pay off as quickly or as easily as it should ... but in my experience, it always pays off. Doing the right thing is *always* the right thing. That doesn't mean it's easy—or painless.

Halloween Candy

When I turned fifty, my doctor encouraged me to go get my first colonoscopy. **Yay.** I dutifully made my appointment.

It was scheduled for November 1. I remember that because it was the day after Halloween and my youngest son—who would have been thirteen at the time—still loved trick-or-treating and savored his candy stash. (He kept it in his room so that his brothers couldn't pilfer it.)

Being single, things like this are hard because you have no spouse to pick you up and you have to have a ride home. I asked a good friend of mine to come get me. She brought me home and made sure I was OK, and then left.

I had never been under anesthesia before and did not know the lingering effects and the amnesia that can occur as you recover. All I remember is that I was tired and went to bed to sleep the afternoon away. When I woke up, the bed was littered with candy wrappers. I had eaten **all** of my son's Halloween candy. But even in that pursuit, I must have fallen asleep because I was kind of wearing a lot of chocolate as well. I must have unwrapped some things and then fallen asleep on top of the candy and rolled around on it. I was covered in chocolate, my bedspread was covered in chocolate, and I can only assume I had consumed thousands of grams of sugar and calories!!

It was hard to explain to a thirteen-year-old exactly what had happened. I don't remember exactly how I explained it, but I was on the hook for replacing **a lot** of candy the next day.

11

Tools for Turns

"Almost everything will work again if you unplug
it for a few minutes, including you."

—Anne Lamott

N o matter who you are or how successful your career has been, it is not uncommon to find yourself adrift—for one reason or another—at some point. It is an uncomfortable place, to be sure. But that doesn't mean that it can't be productive. So many people, given this opportunity, waste it. Paralyzed with anxiety, or escaping into playtime, they essentially tap their foot until the winds change and life moves on. But what I would like to suggest is that there are concrete steps you can take and self-reflection that you can do that might actually accelerate successfully moving into that next chapter. Every situation is different, but the tools presented here are meant to be a starter—a primer—for the types of exercises and thought processes that you may want to consider if you find yourself a bit lost and confused. They may help you to become "unstuck."

My year of unemployment—while filled with insecurity and doubt at first—turned out to be transformative for me. It allowed me so many gifts. The amount of growth and perspective that I gained was life-changing. I ended up focusing on my mind, body, and spirit, although I didn't really even consciously do that—I guess all of those areas just needed to be worked on! To quote Brené Brown,

"'Crazy-busy' is a great armor, it's a great way for numbing. What a lot of us do is that we stay so busy, and so out in front of our life, that the truth of how we're feeling and what we really need can't catch up with us."

The body component was straightforward: After years of anxiety and exhaustion, I took simple steps to relax. I slept better and worked out. I read more and had quiet time. I allowed myself to escape into mindless TV without feeling guilty. I felt like I started to take full breaths again, maybe for the first time ever. And I started a low dose of an antidepressant to treat the tendency toward low-grade depression that persistently dogged me.

In addition to focusing on health, I was able to really dig deep and think about who I truly was from an analytical point of view. I dug into the people-pleasing habit that I had formed. I finally invested in a good therapist to better understand my drive and perfectionist tendencies and where they came from. (Thanks, Mom!) Without the construct of a boss and a job and a husband and my parents, what was I really all about? What was I good at? More importantly—what did I enjoy and how did I find fulfillment? The gift that I had—my ability to "sell" myself into just about anything—stood in stark contrast to my less developed ability to be a "buyer." How could I learn to discern what was a good fit for me—not just from a résumé-building aspect, but through an authenticity lens?

In a sense, it was hard work. Learning yourself at forty years old is a challenge—there are so many long-ingrained habits and perspectives. But it was also stimulating, and actually encouraging. I spent a great deal of time that year exploring living and leadership philosophies and adopted some that I use to this day. For example, one advisor told me that all people—regardless of the specific circumstances—have a tendency to be comfortable using two out of three modalities: acting, thinking, or feeling. We all tend to have a dominant and a secondary proclivity. But the key to understanding yourself and overcoming your own shortcomings is to force yourself to do the third one—the one that is *not* naturally comfortable for you. For me, it was clear that I am thinking, followed by acting. I tend to subjugate my feelings. Which is why, if I force myself to slow down and "feel the feelings," I tend to make better decisions.

When I have used this construct, time and time again in both personal and business environments, I have observed that a lot of my friends and colleagues—unlike myself—tend to be feeling first, then thinking—or vice versa, thinking first, then feeling. Either way, it's a loop of being inside your own head. The result of this is that no action gets taken and they get stuck. For them, taking action—almost any action—moves them off the dime and starts them on a path to progress. It is really helpful to assess yourself and understand how you fit within this approach, and to see where you can really improve yourself to get better outcomes.

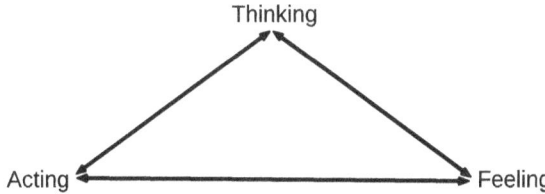

I also became very familiar with the Enneagram—a personality test that will evaluate you and place you in one of nine personality types. It is quite advanced and I found it to be eerily insightful for me. I learned that I am a "loyalist" (which explains the people-pleasing!), and that under pressure I devolve into being an "overachiever," which I did repeatedly up until this point in my life. But at my best, I elevate to being a "peacemaker" . . . which coincidentally is what I have morphed into being as my career has advanced and I have gained confidence. In my board leadership evolution, for example, I have found that in the chair role I have truly morphed into my authentic self. I love every element of that role and it supports my highest personality elevation. No longer "striving," the role of mediating to get to consensus and integrating alternative points of views is, in a business sense, becoming a peacemaker.

It is highly likely that with whatever kind of circumstances led to your displacement, it will prompt you to think long and hard about why you were at the company you were with—and what signs you could have seen coming before you got smacked by the prevailing winds. Even in the worst of existential crises, I would observe that the folks who are a really good fit, who really excel at their jobs, do not tend to get let go. So some reflection around "fit" seems natural as you try to accept and reconcile things. With that in mind, I think there is a paradigm that measures "fit" across two axes: time and place. Take a look at the following matrix. In a four-quadrant graph, fully functioning people are usually in the upper-right corner of *right place, right time*; while clear misfits are in the lower-left corner of *wrong place, wrong time*. But what if things aren't so clear? What if you need to decipher what exactly didn't work for you? Was it the place? Or the time? Here are some ways to think about that.

For me, this graphical depiction really helped me to discern the "when to stay, when to go" conundrum. I came up with a matrix:

Right/Wrong Time/Place Matrix

Right Time

Upper-left quadrant (Wrong Place, Right Time):
- Your mind, body, and lifestyle support being able to do this
- You are energized but sad at the same time
- You are not on the same page as others regarding values

Upper-right quadrant (Right Place, Right Time):
- You have a high energy level
- You feel like you contribute
- You feel validated and supported
- You are aligned with others on your values
- You feel that you can bring your authentic self to work

Wrong Place ← → **Right Place**

Lower-left quadrant (Wrong Place, Wrong Time):
- You are very unhappy
- You have a very high level of stress
- You feel overwhelmed and out of control
- You can't see any avenue to make it work

Lower-right quadrant (Right Place, Wrong Time):
- You have the talent
- You have the energy
- You feel like you (could) fit
- Something isn't clicking

Wrong Time

Questions to ask yourself:

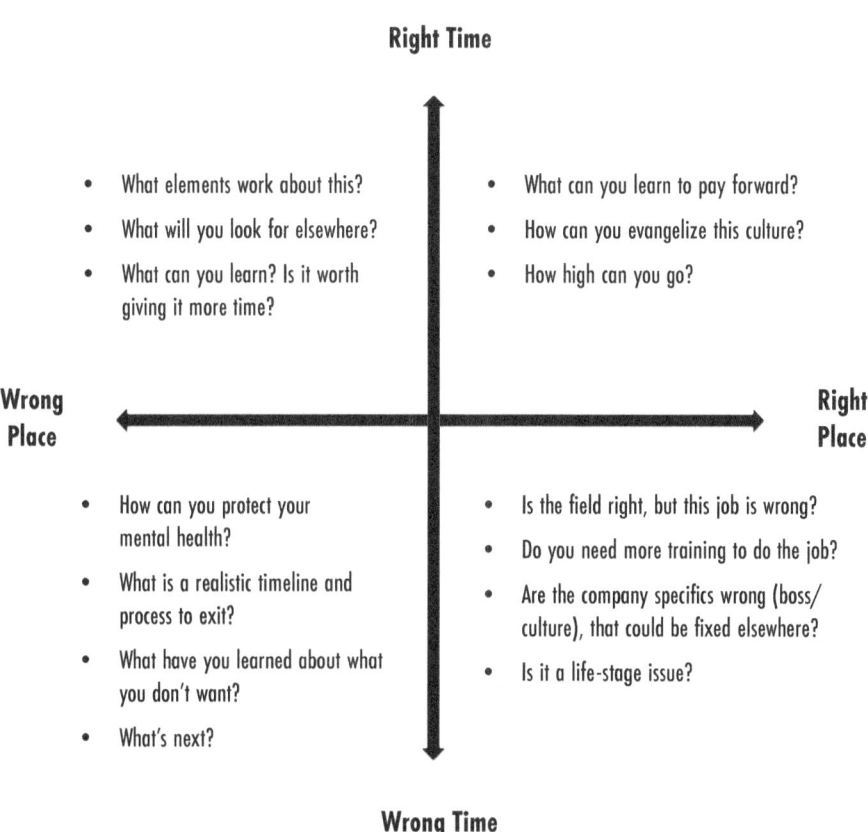

Right Time

- What elements work about this?
- What will you look for elsewhere?
- What can you learn? Is it worth giving it more time?

- What can you learn to pay forward?
- How can you evangelize this culture?
- How high can you go?

Wrong Place

Right Place

- How can you protect your mental health?
- What is a realistic timeline and process to exit?
- What have you learned about what you don't want?
- What's next?

- Is the field right, but this job is wrong?
- Do you need more training to do the job?
- Are the company specifics wrong (boss/culture), that could be fixed elsewhere?
- Is it a life-stage issue?

Wrong Time

I really think you will clearly identify with one of these situations, so trust your gut, and use these questions to help discern the mistakes and pledge **not** to repeat them as you find your next role.

I also dabbled in self-help psychology, which provided so many new ways of thinking. It helped me to get grounded and more philosophical about business and the role it plays in my life. There are all kinds of tools out there and the trick is to find the ones that work for you. For me, it became about redefining what "planning" looked like (since all of my plans had worked out so well up to that point!). I chose to focus on life and not work. I thought about and started to define my bucket list—not for titles or dollars, but for experiences and impact. (See my "Bucket List" at the end of this book.)

I ultimately decided that within the work world, I wanted to help to build healthy workplace cultures and to be a force for good in my C-suite roles. I especially wanted to be a support for women, in particular single moms. That mattered more to me than where I worked or who I worked for or what industry I was in. And it was great to get that clarity. Learning to focus on the greater good and less on yourself can be very freeing. And it allows me today to take steps to make a difference, including writing this book. I have done dozens of fireside chats around the country with women's groups to tell my story and try to demystify the corporate ladder and career success, as well as learning to balance competing priorities. It gives me great joy to share this and to try to help people. I have a handful of handwritten notes and emails from people telling me that my story really helped them and made them feel less alone. I like that.

In terms of spirit, I dabbled in some metaphysical studies and thought very philosophically about how to approach my life. I thought hard about what elements of existence would add a healthy construct for me to have as foundations—"filters" if you will—that would guide me. I thought about specific words, in particular, and I settled on eight that would build a pyramid-type construct for the rest of my life. I still use it today. For me, the most basic level includes the following: security, integrity, and divinity. If I have those three elements in my life, I feel grounded. If those are met, then I prioritize choices and experiences that will bring me the next three because they keep me engaged and growing: learning, service, creativity. And if all six of those are present in my life, then I believe I will affect the top tier and have these two: beauty, harmony.

Think about your dreams and priorities and come up with your own "life words."

This construct came to be a guide for what changes to make. I know, for example, that I care a lot about my home and having a serene and attractive environment. I think better and feel calmer. Similarly, I realized that I am not conflict-avoidant generally—which is good because you need that in leadership. But I also realized that I do not like or want conflict in my personal life. That is difficult for me and can really weigh me down.

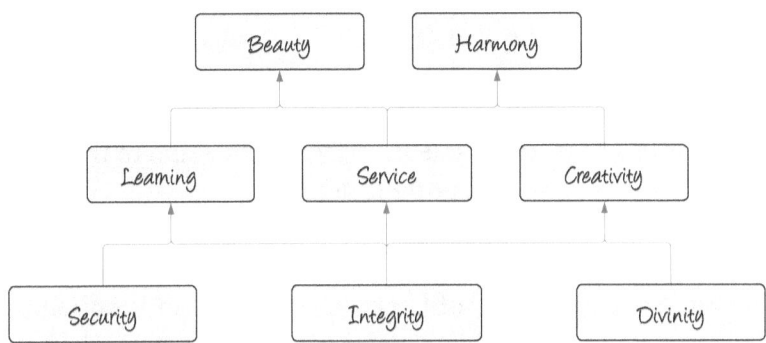

Around this time, I began both spending time and money to improve my home décor *and* I began pruning unhealthy relationships from my life. Toxic friendships and friendships based on obligation or merely shared histories that were fraught were gently eliminated. I decided to observe which relationships were truly reciprocal, and the ones that were one-sided were pushed aside. I became more protective of my time and energy. I adopted Maya Angelou's "Believe people when they tell you who they are" adage. I just became much clearer about where I spent my time and effort, prioritizing my children and my healthier friendships.

The more I learned about myself, the more confident I became about treating myself better and finding balance between what I wanted and what I needed to do for my family. And the subsequent sacrifices that I decided to make for my family in the years to come came much more easily and without resentment, because in other ways, I was taking better care of myself.

But concurrent with all of this was the fact that I needed to find a job—and I had no idea what that would look like. I wasn't sure I wanted to be a CFO, or even really to stay in finance. At first, I tried to think about finding another job quickly, since living off of savings made me nervous. But I honestly just couldn't figure out where to go from where I found myself. I had had career successes for sure, and despite the setbacks, I had continued to climb the corporate ladder. Becoming a public company CFO at thirty-nine years old—even if it was a complete disaster—was something to be proud of. It was also a cautionary tale never to be repeated. And it certainly had not been a smooth road that I had traveled. I promised myself I would never again "jump" at the chance for a higher salary or impressive title simply because it dazzled me, nor would I take the easiest way out. I simply had to become smarter, shrewder, and much more selective in how I was going to offer my talents to the world—and to truly believe that I had them—and not let others define me.

It sounds small but it was a BIG lesson for me. Think about it—I went to Duke because they accepted me into a unique program and I was flattered, I went to U of C because my husband wanted me to stay in Chicago, I took the bank and the accounting firm jobs because they easily solved an employment problem without much effort on my part, and the list continued—I always took the easy answer or accepted a new role because I was surprised and flattered. That year, for the first time, I had the time and space to stop, to ponder, to evaluate and grow.

A friend of mine said, "You are in your own garden—tend to your garden." I loved the analogy. A garden is beautiful, peaceful, yet productive. That was my year off. It also became clear to me that when you tend to your own garden, you are learning to advocate for yourself and to think for yourself—which, in turn, makes you much less dependent on outside validation. So I came up with a meditation that I still love that allows me to quickly take stock of all of the important areas in my life from time to time. And it is based on the concept of tending to this imaginary garden that represents my life.

In my mind it takes place in a beautiful yard of a building in Chicago that I know. I close my eyes and imagine taking a walk to different parts of my garden. There is a section for friends, partnership, health, career, and money; I would walk around to each area to water it and see what shape it was in. I remember back when I was single, my friends section was beautiful and fragrant and I didn't need to water it much because it had so many nutrients. Then I would walk to the partnership section and it was like a patch of dead weeds. Taking stock of each area showed where more personal investment was needed, and also showed polarities that needed to be addressed. Over time, at every different stage of my journey, the garden would shift. It is a great way to reflect and think about what parts of your garden need to be tended to and I always found that helpful. And it is always changing, always shifting. This meditation can be dramatically different even months apart.

The challenge, though, especially if you are a thinker/feeler or feeler/thinker, is figuring out *how* to fix the areas that need attention. That is the hard work and it takes patience and time. You need to realize that you can't change everything at once or it won't be sustainable. And change takes time, because improvement doesn't happen overnight. Small baby steps, consistently applied, will yield progress over time. It's the attention and intention that count.

As my self-awareness and confidence grew, and the calm descended on me in those months, I found that I started to listen to an inner voice more. Gone was the voice in my head that had dogged me up until that point. Gone was the need for outside validation and flattery. Even though I was coming from a place of weakness from a classic résumé perspective, I ironically felt stronger than I ever had before.

Yet, the answer to "what's next," after all this reflecting, didn't come easily or quickly. I tested my own ability and counsel to be patient, one of the hardest lessons of that year. Sometimes it seemed like the harder I tried to find the answer, the more elusive it became. And my ideas vacillated wildly from going back into a traditional financial role to becoming an interior designer. I had dozens of informational meetings, talking to many people in my professional and personal sphere. We chatted about who they were and what they did and how they approached their jobs. At times it was overwhelming; at times it was intriguing. Mostly, it was confusing.

And of course, life continued through this year. The boys were growing up. My ex and I learned to partner together for the kids. My friends offered great support—fun escape when I needed it, a shoulder to cry on occasionally, and plenty of chances to unwind and laugh a bit. While it was clear from the beginning that it was only a stopping point along a much longer journey, it was such a special time. I wish everyone could take a mid-career sabbatical, regardless of the circumstances that lead them there—to pause, to rest, to regroup, and to restore. Even if it feels potentially catastrophic at the time, trust that it is a moment in time and that a career is decades long. A pause in the action is simply that ... a pause. Embrace it.

I do not think it is coincidence (nor do I think it was dumb luck) that coming out of that year, I made changes and selections that proved wildly successful. Of course, that didn't mean there wouldn't be challenges ahead; there are always challenges and growth. But I was so much better about applying the lessons I had learned and I found that the universe rewarded me in ways I never could have hoped for or imagined. My "plans" had repeatedly either led me down the wrong path or had blown up in various ways. Only when I stopped trying to manufacture "plans" did things start to fall into place.

Boiling down a year's worth of reflection, I essentially determined that there were going to have to be some nonnegotiables from that point on. In no particular order, they were:

1. I would never put myself in a position where I felt alone, isolated, and exposed again. I wanted to have support to go to when times get tough.

2. I wanted some flexibility to work when I needed to work, but to have personal time when I needed it also, so that I could be a better mother.

3. I wanted my skills and efforts to be appreciated and valued.

4. As much as an interior design career sounded fun—I needed a certain level of salary to support my iron-clad commitment to my children and their education which, in Chicago, meant private schools.

It's funny how the universe works. In the end, the answer materialized slowly, as if puzzle pieces started to stand out and then fit together. And that in and of itself is a lesson ... blinding flashes of brilliance (or the obvious) don't often happen. A slow dawning is more common and less blatantly clear. Across several weeks and from very different social sources, the name of one firm kept being mentioned. None of the people mentioning it knew much about it. It was a Southeastern company that was opening a Chicago office. They were an equity partnership of experienced CFOs who did turnaround interim assignments for companies needing help. Their niche was to find small to midsized private and public companies that could not afford or did not have sophisticated financial leadership experience in-house—but that needed such expertise in the short term. For me, while it wasn't exactly a eureka moment, the concept intrigued me and so I found the name of the new Chicago managing partner and called him.

Our initial conversation was quite tentative on both sides. I was not sure I ever wanted to be a CFO again, and he understandably was not exactly blown away by my résumé. But we continued to have conversations over several months. On my side, the conclusion that I wanted this came as much from a lack of other appealing options at the time, to grudgingly acknowledging that it had the potential to meet all of my nonnegotiables. As an interim CFO, you were only paid when you worked for a client; in between you had no income and you were supposed to do marketing on behalf of the partnership to keep the pipeline full—even if the future beneficiaries of that work might be your partners. So the income stream could be bumpy . . . but it was also very lucrative when you were engaged, enough so to make up for the down times.

In addition, although the marketing requirement existed while in between engagements, the down time was pretty free and I thought those times would be good for me to spend more time as a mom and recuperating a bit from the stresses of what were surely going to be high-stress situations. As an equity partner in the firm, I would also have a chance to build meaningful wealth if the company continued to grow. And, when situations got tough, I would have partners and peers to go to for support and guidance. I had stopped thinking, if I ever had at all, about long-term plans and aspirations. I was thinking more practically and more shrewdly now. So I decided this could be the right next step.

I am not completely familiar with the twelve-step program but I nevertheless have great respect for it for the millions who have used it to change their lives. And I know that within the twelve steps, they focus people away from the end game since it can seem too remote and impossible. Instead, they just tell them to focus on the next right step, then the one after that, etc. Focusing on just the next step and figuring you'll figure it out from there has become my mantra. And it was certainly the way I approached joining this firm.

My affiliation lasted eleven years with this company and I not only did extremely well—I actually never had downtime. I ended up becoming head of the CFO practice which, by that point, had grown to over three hundred CFOs nationwide as equity partners. The value of the firm grew handsomely over those eleven years. More importantly, I was happy, I was thriving, and I absolutely loved being part of that company. I was proud to be a partner in that firm.

I will never forget at my fiftieth birthday party, the Chicago managing partner whom I had worked directly for all of those years gave a toast. In it he said, "I hired her by a fifty-point-one percent margin and I believe she accepted equally doubtfully!" He was absolutely right—it had been a tentative decision. I was unsure if I had what it took to do that job well, and I know that he had doubts as well. But he gave me a chance—with my one ten-month disastrous stint as a CFO, he saw something in me and gave me another chance. I didn't fully appreciate it at the time, and it likely might never have happened if he hadn't been building a new business, but he changed my professional life profoundly and I am forever grateful. His name is Dirk Landis—and, yes, that is his real name. I am proud to be associated with him.

Recently when I was being interviewed in a fireside chat, someone in the audience asked me who I go to for advice and counsel. As I thought about it, I realized that, while I have wonderful friends and business colleagues to ask about specific topics, mostly at this point in my life I keep my own counsel. I have seen so much and lived through so many different situations that I trust, with some time and reflection (and perhaps the right glass of wine), I can come to my own conclusions and trust what comes to me. That is a real gift and I think it started that year, when I took the time to dig deep and reorient myself.

Taking a Tumble

I had a several-hour-long conference call one day, when I led the CFO practice and was doing my public-speaking gigs. My home office was on the lowest floor of my house with a bath and laundry on the half floor above. I was scheduled to speak in the back half of the call on a complex topic that was expected to last about thirty minutes. In the first half of the call, I decided to give myself a bio break and ran up the curved flight of stairs to the bathroom.

While I was peeing, I heard my name called. (**Damn! Had they accelerated the agenda?**)

I quickly stood up—a little too quickly if you catch my drift—and ran for the stairs. I slipped at the top of the stairs and fell all the way down, slamming my foot when I landed. (My head and arm weren't in great shape either!) I lay there in a daze while I processed the fact that they hadn't even been calling on me to present—they had only made a passing reference to me as part of another conversation. So I hobbled up two flights of stairs to my kitchen and grabbed a frozen bag of peas and went back downstairs to the call.

While I waited for the designated time for my presentation, my foot kept swelling and I kept getting lightheaded. I ended up doing the presentation half sitting/reclining so I could put my head down (PowerPoint on the floor in front of me) while my foot was elevated with the frozen peas on top of it ... yes, I looked like a contortionist!

The problem was that just after the call, I needed to head to the airport to give a speech the next day. I popped a few Percocet pills that I'd had from a prior surgery and hailed a cab to the airport. The most amusing part, in retrospect, was that once at the airport I was relatively pain-free thanks to the pills—but I also had a really hard time focusing. I'd read each display for my gate, walk about twenty feet, and then realize I'd already forgotten what gate I was walking to. I read display after display until I finally made it to my gate and boarded my flight.

Once I landed, they had someone assigned to pick me up and act as my concierge for the time I was there. She was great and took me to my hotel with the promise to pick me up the next morning when I was supposed to speak. I told her I had taken a "slight tumble" in case she noticed I was limping a bit. Well, the next morning my ankle was swollen to the size somewhere between a baseball and a basketball and it was extremely discolored. She was aghast when she met me in the lobby and noticed that I'd shoved my very swollen foot into a three-inch-high heel.

I'm sure she was a mom because she took one look and said, "We are going directly from your speech to the hospital. I don't care when your flight is or what your plans are, you are not leaving here until we get that checked out."

And sure enough—after I awkwardly gave my speech—she took me to the emergency room and they confirmed that, of course, my foot was broken and I was given a boot for six weeks. And it was with that boot that I then flew from there to my son's college graduation!

12

BFFs

"Friendship is a wildly underrated medication."

—Anna Deavere Smith

riendships are a tricky business in the best of times. While completely essential to a happy life, they can also surprise, disappoint, hurt, and confuse. Mostly they should delight. Since human nature is by definition involved, they are ever changing, emotionally complex, and a delicate balancing act. From an early age I invested in friendships; being somewhat lonely as a kid and under my mother's thumb, I yearned for conversation outside of my house. I enjoyed spending time with my friends' families—even traveling with them occasionally. These relationships fed me and expanded my worldview, my appreciation for diversity, and my travel horizons.

Yet, even then at times, they were painful. In sixth grade I was bullied at a new private school that I had just started attending. I made new friends and started off well, I thought. Middle school girls are notoriously mean, I suppose because they are trying to understand their place in the pecking order of life. But for whatever reason, some of these new "friends" decided to call my house over a series of nights (with thinly disguised voices), saying things like "Cindie, you're mean and ugly and everybody hates you." I was scared, upset, and confused. I barely knew these girls. Why did they hate me so much? My parents were alarmed as well, and none of us felt very good about this new school. I suppose my parents reported it because I know at some point, they decided to pull me (midyear) out of that school and send me to the local public school.

But, even through that misery, there was growth—and that is worth reflecting on. My father put me to bed one night in the midst of this and said, "I want you to be happy at your new school [the public one I was moving to]. And I am sorry all of this happened—you don't deserve it. *If you were a boy I would make you stay and fight it out—but, honey, let's just get you out of there.*"

Wait. WHAT? I will never forget the way those words landed. *No way. I'm not leaving. If you would make a boy stay and gut it out then you should make me do that too.*

I completely changed my attitude. I refused to leave. And I thought about what I could do to change the situation. I went back to that school and actively cultivated new friends. It was tough; it was one of my earlier grit-producing experiences. I never directly confronted the two girls who had called (it was easy to figure out who they were), but I completely ignored them until, a few months later, they came sucking up to me. I'm not going to lie—that was gratifying! And instructional. How fickle is middle school? If you don't overreact, and move on, things often sort themselves out. I gracefully accepted their friendship but never trusted them again. At the end of that year—at which point I *did* change schools—I had a yearbook full of love notes, including from those two girls. How very Anne of Cleves! And so ... yes, we can learn a lot from friends and frenemies.

One of the reasons I include that story—because there are tons of kids who have had a bullying episode in their youth—is to point out that you have to learn how to be a friend and how to pick a friend. Like anything in life, you do that by trial and error. You make mistakes, you get hurt. You rebound. You get pickier. The sooner you learn it, the less pain and drain is involved. And one of the reasons that people-pleasing is so hard is that it is draining. Instead of drawing boundaries and protecting yourself, you spend countless hours doing things for other people and sparing their feelings at the expense of your own. Those are not good friends!

I have gone on to form true friendships—lifelong, soul-affirming friendships—albeit not many. But really—how many of those do you need? You are lucky if you find two or three in a lifetime. Treasure them! So few go the distance through the twists and turns and ups and downs of life. My very best friend is Fraser. Fraser and I have known each other for decades now. We met at the consumer products company where he was a "star" brand manager and I was his financial analyst. He went through the Pete experience with me and was one of the reasons I stayed sane through that; it could have ended there once I moved on. But Fraser has remained my go-to, tell-anything-to person ever since. Why? So many reasons: He is wise, he "gets" me, he isn't judging, he will gently push back and tell me what I need to hear; he is forgiving, and importantly, we see the world the same way. And we laugh, *oh*, do we laugh. Ironically, Fraser and I rarely connect. Neither of us like the phone much and we are both very busy. We live in different cities and we are both married now. Maybe after so many years we just have an understood cadence. But I'll tell you—if I need him, he is there. When he reaches out, I respond immediately. He even spoke at my son's wedding—my son and daughter-in-law's choice with no prompting from me.

I have others, but I use Fraser as an example to point out what I think are the key elements to lasting friendships. A foundational one is doing the work, making the investment. You only have bandwidth to be *that* friend to a few. Fraser has always invested in our relationship. He shows up no matter how painful, inconvenient, or messy it is to do so. I have learned the hard way that things have to go both ways. I have no patience or room in my life anymore for one-way friendships.

But I have plenty of solid, real friendships that I cherish, that feed me, challenge me, and lift me up. They come from all different chapters and places in my life. Some last for many years. My friend DeAnn talks about delineating between being friends in the trenches versus "real" friends. But friends in the trenches (i.e., friends you bond with in a memorable situation, but not permanently) can be critically important—and I have deep affection for many people who I've shared tough corporate or motherhood moments with; those friends are really there for you in a time and a place when you need them. Sometimes they last for years and years. But for whatever reason, they don't last a lifetime. They never get to that deepest level. And that's OK—life changes and moves on. Circumstances change.

I should amend that: That's OK, *sometimes*. But some friendships and lost connections you genuinely mourn, even though you recognize they need to go. That can be hard. I had two really close friends growing up—like, high-school-girl-talk-on-the-phone-every-night-for-an-hour friends. They lasted for years and years and I really thought both would last for life. But each had a falling out, and to this day I can't really understand either one. One went through a painful divorce, and lashed out in anger, saying that I didn't offer enough support. Maybe she didn't remember that I had just gone through the same? Maybe I didn't support her, I don't remember; perhaps I was triggered. The other reacted very bizarrely to a letter that I wrote expressing condolences when her mother died. I was very sad about the passing because I had grown up spending a lot of time in their house and had a lot of memories to share. I thought it would comfort her, make her smile. So I talked about my memories. And to my shock and disappointment, she wrote back that my letter was selfish and "all about me."

Here's the thing—friendships require forgiveness, if they are going to go the distance. The friend who went through the divorce? Well we had a pinky promise in high school that when we got married, we would be in each other's weddings. I went first and kept my end of the bargain—she was my maid of honor. When she got married a few years later I got a simple wedding invitation—and no phone call to even explain the slight. It hurt, but I let it go.

When our high school reunion came around more than a decade later, I decided to be the bigger person and emailed her. OK—I told a white lie and wrote something like, "I don't really remember why we lost touch, but it would be great to see you again!" She responded— oh, did she respond. Three paragraphs about how I didn't support her adequately when she got divorced and *that* was why and she was *shocked* I didn't remember. She was by then (I had heard) happily remarried with two kids. I skipped the reunion (there were only about fifty people in our graduating class)—not out of fear but out of disgust. Forgive; move on; let go. But don't volunteer for the abuse. Come on.

The friend who didn't like the condolence letter? Well, she did come around again—our birthdays are one day apart and the following year, she emailed me on my birthday with a sweet, kind not-exactly-an-apology, but warm remembrance. I embraced it. We talked again for a while until another episode occurred; it was once again a "review" of something I had said or how I'd said it. That was it for me. It was right around this time that I found one of my favorite (anonymous) quotes, "If you're not changing your friends from time to time, you're not growing." And I believe in second chances—just not endless chances.

Melissa Kirsch, a provocative columnist for the *New York Times*, wrote a column titled "Renewed Resolve" on February 1, 2025. In it, she explores a list of "prompts, topics for journaling, ideas for reconsidering how you're living or not living." The part of the column that struck me was the following: "PHANTOM LIMB: Name something you miss but—if offered—you don't actually want back." Provocative indeed! And as I reflected on that prompt, I realized that some of these expired friendships fall into that category. On some level I miss them; I mourn them. But in reality I honestly wouldn't choose to have them back! They didn't work for specific reasons and those reasons would not have gone away.

But let's focus specifically on work friends for a moment. It would be hard to go somewhere every work day, interact with people all day long, and not begin to form attachments. This is especially true in high-stress situations; people need to connect to survive. But work environments are fraught. Hierarchies complicate things; competitiveness can get in the way. And you will only know in hindsight if a friendship is a "trench" friendship . . . most likely it is. So I would counsel assuming that even friendships with great chemistry are trench relationships, at least until they can stand some test of time. Trust slowly. Like an onion, peel it back layer by layer.

Be alert to signs that people are politically motivated. Are they pumping you for information? Are they unusually "interested" in your work life, but not your home life? Can they remember your work deadline, but not your kids' names? I have had several experiences with advisors—one lawyer and one investment banker, as examples—with whom I thought I was genuinely close. We talked about kids, travel, spouses; we frequently went out socially. Yet, when I changed jobs or was no longer useful to them, they disappeared. It's always sad to realize that someone loved your title ... not you.

I also learned the hard way that there has to be a bright red line when you are in a position to know information that your friend doesn't. And the higher you climb, the more common this becomes. I had an experience very early in my career when we were planning layoffs but had not announced them yet. A friend was panic stricken by the rumors and feared being let go. She was in a different division, but I had knowledge of the list and knew that she wasn't on it. So I told her—to be kind, and to put her out of her misery. She never asked me; I volunteered it. It was on me. Because although she *was* grateful and relieved, she also blurted it out in a meeting with her boss. What had I done? Without thinking it through, I had, first, confirmed the fact that there were going to be layoffs and, second, put myself at risk by assuming that she would keep her mouth shut. She didn't. I was questioned about it and fessed up—I almost lost my job. I certainly lost my credibility and was not included in confidential briefings for a long time. I never forgot that lesson. I had to cultivate a way to be friends while enforcing boundaries. I adopted an approach where I would say to my friends, "You can ask me anything. I will tell you if I can't comment and you'll have to respect that ... but I will never, ever lie to you."

The other old adage that is so true is that it is lonely at the top. I had a conversation recently with a general counsel who said to me, "I love the people I work with, but I can't get too close because I never know who I'll have to investigate." And he and I shared a cynical chuckle at that because, in fact, I had had to lead an investigation into him at one point when he was falsely accused of an ethical breach. I said, "Yup—you're right. You never know who you'll have to investigate." And that brings up another aspect of the politics involved: The higher you go, the more people can be out to get you. I have known several people, myself included (see the "No Thanks" story after Chapter 16), who are bizarrely and falsely accused of all sorts of things and the right governance is to investigate to absolutely ensure that there is no truth to it. But most are honestly a waste of time and are selfishly motivated. As an audit chair, I have led six investigations related to accusations of: earnings manipulation, unexpected account-ing charges, employee embezzlement and arrest, racial discrimination, and supposed CEO ethical violations (twice). So, yes, it's hard enough to do that without the added complexity of a personal relationship.

So tread lightly—but don't completely shy away from exploring a relationship with someone you have a connection with at work. There are so many good people out there who are fun, smart, entertaining, trustworthy, and worth the risk. But be smart about it! And even though work friendships are valuable, make sure they are not your only avenue to find the trust and comfort that true friends can pro-vide. Work-life balance applies to more than just how you spend your time.

It seems counterintuitive and overly prescriptive to share "rules" for friendships, so I will simply offer you my "thoughts" on how to select and maintain healthy friendships—acquaintances, cowork-ers, trench friends, and life friends. My hope is that perhaps it will encourage you to evaluate and elevate yours. After all, that is one part of your "garden" that needs to be examined and watered.

- Be as kind, accepting, and forgiving to your friend as you would like them to be to you.

- Learn to share your most private thoughts slowly; trust builds over time and shortcuts can be a recipe for disaster.

- Let things go; everyone has a bad day from time to time.

- If there is a rift, take some time to decide if you really want to heal it. If so, reach out and talk it out—friendships will go through ups and downs. If not, accept you are not a good fit.

- Give space—friendships are measured in the quality of moments of love and support, not the quantity of moments together.

- Ask for what you need—friends are not mind readers.

- Don't ask for too much too frequently—in other words, don't be needy. Save it for when you really need a friend and only **that** friend will do.

- Objectively assess if you are the one doing all of the work and investment; if so, it's time to go.

- Be there when your friend needs you. (I learned that one the hard way.)

- Notice how time passes when you're with them—it should be fast!

- Look to see if you are walking on eggshells around them—you should be comfortable and completely yourself in a "safe" friendship.

- Don't get greedy, and don't overextend and get resentful.

- Accept that long-term friendships can grow and change and go through multiple phases—they are living, growing organisms.

- Be truly grateful that these people came into your life.

I also will note for the record the difference between male and female friendships (in general). It is profound. Women often share so much more, get really personal, and in my opinion, can really sustain each other through tough times. We confide our weaknesses; we share our vulnerabilities. Living as much as I do in a man's world, I observe the companionship and shared interests that men bond over. But they seem to fall into only a few categories: work, sports, hobbies. I do not think that most men are comfortable being vulnerable around each other. And that perhaps leads them to be more emotionally dependent on their wives or partners.

I like that I have honest, authentic support from a number of people—and I have a choice of whom I go to, depending on the issue. If it is a medical issue (which I can be quite neurotic about), I call my sisters—both in medicine, both highly empathetic, and both know what

I need to hear (massive amounts of reassurance). My husband does not have the ability to do that—not being neurotic himself, about that anyway—he usually rolls his eyes, makes a dismissive comment, and tells me to call my doctor. Very practical. Not helpful. But if I have a business issue to untangle? He is the best. Other girlfriends are great for any frustrations I might have with my kids; others for frustrations I have in my relationship—still others are fantastic lunch partners to rail about politics, geopolitical fears, or climate change. Man, it takes a village to keep me sane, fully functioning, and balanced. And my friends do that for me.

Garden Party

Janice Ellig is a top-notch executive recruiter that I have worked with both as a client (looking to hire) and as a candidate. I have known her for years and even sit on her advisory board. She specializes in diversity placements for the C-suite and the board. She works with dozens (hundreds?) of companies and brings a unique approach to search for, vet, and eventually place people into new roles. She is also a bit of an institution in New York City, where her company is based. She has been involved for years as the creator of the Breakfast of Champions, an event held in NYC to recognize companies whose boards are composed of 40 percent (or more) women. Several hundred top executives from the very top companies in the nation attend it.

To my mind she is a master networker—one of those people who seems to know everyone. How she has the time to do so much for so many is beyond me.

Anyway, many years ago when I was just starting to get to know her, she generously invited me to attend a party that she and her husband, Bruce, were hosting in their house. Her parties are legendary—quite large and a cast of "who's who" in attendance. And she promotes interaction—her rule is you have to leave one of her parties having talked to five people you didn't know before that night. I was flattered.

I took the subway to the Upper East Side and started walking toward her address. As the streets got smaller and smaller, it was obvious that another woman was headed the same way. We introduced ourselves and laughed that—both attending our first "Janice" party—meeting outside the building counted as one of the five people we needed to meet during the course of the evening.

Now, Janice lives in a very elegant building with a vintage elevator (at least at that point), personally operated by an elevator attendant. When my new friend and I got in the elevator, the attendant said, "Party, right?"

"Yes, sir!" we said in unison.

So up we went and the elevator opened into a beautiful apartment with a few dozen people deep into their cocktails and hors d'oeuvres. We entered; we split up; we started mingling. Everyone was very friendly, but I remember thinking that my usual business-oriented cocktail chitchat wasn't quite landing. Still—whatever ... over the next hour I had two glasses of wine and some food and mingled my ass off.

I think I was on number three, in terms of the people I needed to meet, when my new friend came running across the room looking panic stricken. She grabbed my arm and said, "Put your drink down—we are at the wrong party!"

It turns out there were two parties in Janice's small, refined building that night—one was Janice's on a much higher floor and the other was the Upper East Side Gardening Society which I was, in fact, attending. No wonder none of my board chitchat was landing. No wonder people who kept asking me about my favorite flowers and referring to famous public gardens were stumped by my lack of responses.

We got back in the elevator—the attendant apologized profusely (and laughed)—and we headed up to Janice's. It was larger and very busy there, and I am not sure to this day if Janice realized how late I was or has ever heard this story—she will now!

13

Impostor Syndrome

"I still have a little impostor syndrome. . . . It doesn't go away, that feeling that you shouldn't take me that seriously. What do I know?"

—Michelle Obama

A h, impostor syndrome. So many of us have it. Even Michelle Obama, apparently, and she is the very definition of badass, in my opinion. I wonder if Anne of Cleves felt it too? Yes, it's hard to describe—but, again, like Supreme Court Justice Potter Stewart's definition of porn: "I know it when I see it." Let's take a hard look at it.

The term was coined by psychologists Pauline Rose Clance and Suzanne Imes in a 1978 study that looked at high-achieving people who consistently believed themselves to be less bright or talented than the world thought they were. Since then, it has exploded into popular culture and is often claimed, usually by women, interestingly enough. As a matter of fact, when I told my CEO husband I was going to add a chapter in this book about it, he said, "What's that?" Seriously. He is married to a woman who has been consistently plagued by it, as have his daughters, and yet he had no clue.

According to a systemic review by Bravata et al., published in the *Journal of Mental Health & Clinical Psychology*, studies have found that up to 82 percent of people experience it at some time (depending on the screening method and studied population), and it is especially prevalent in minorities. A potentially large risk factor for becoming susceptible to it is coming from a family that highly emphasizes achievement.

So what is it exactly? Again . . . hard to define, but here are the symptoms:

- You constantly compare yourself to others.

- You critique yourself constantly.

- You are haunted by your mistakes.

- You worry that others think you are not measuring up.

- You overprepare routinely—yet still feel anxiety.

- The **Sunday Scaries** keep you company every single weekend.

- You feel little to no agency—paralyzed and filled with doubt.

And apparently there are five subtypes: *the perfectionist, the superhero, the expert, the natural genius,* and *the soloist.* It is easy to research this if it speaks to you. Suffice it to say, you will recognize your type when you do. I fall into the superhero category—no pressure there!

A little bit of impostor syndrome, I would argue, is good—even healthy. As my friend Sebastian said to me once in a board meeting, "Everyone in here is an insecure overachiever." It's true. Insecurity can be motivating—it can nudge you to study harder, prepare better, and work smarter to produce that competitive edge. But a little goes a long way. The problem is when you carry it in your pocket every day, everywhere. That can be bad—*very* bad. The biggest danger of impostor syndrome is that, left unchecked, it can become a self-fulfilling prophecy. And the *last* thing you need is to become your own worst enemy. Your anxiety can get to the point where it impacts your performance.

Consider an easy example: You check and recheck your work and rewrite every email—so much so that your work is keeping people waiting. Or you get so tongue tied with indecision that you don't speak up in meetings. Confidence (real or faked) is important. It builds trust and credibility. Authority. No one will put you in a position of authority if you've never displayed it.

There are other downsides to too much impostor syndrome—it can cause unnecessary job-hopping. And unfortunately, that usually occurs because you gave yourself your own performance review—without validation or confirmation from the outside. In anticipation of forecasted humiliation, you pack your bags, outrunning it until the next time. But most of all, let's face it, this is no way to live! Chronic anxiety is one of the most uncomfortable, debilitating states of mind to suffer—especially daily. I know. That year in the garden helped me to reflect on that and quit it cold-turkey.

How does one get out of their head and out of their own way? I found it helpful to ask yourself these three questions: *Is it really the job? Is it really my performance? Is it really me?*

1. **Is it really the job?** Any sane person would question their performance, not to mention their sanity, if they are working for a bad boss (like Pete or Tim)—bosses who thrive on keeping you off-balance. Narcissists who purposely tell you that **you** are the problem. Likewise, a toxic culture or an overly competitive environment can foster insecurity and doubt. In those instances, you are not crazy—just a victim.

2. **Is it really my performance?** Are you in the wrong job? Are you inadequately trained or managed? Are expectations unreasonable? One of my sons was given a performance goal to start a new consulting practice and have twelve active clients at the end of the first quarter. Impossible. Period. Just one real-world example of how someone can be made to feel inadequate before they even start a project. The psychological impact of impossible standards and goals is profound. Or maybe you are just not a good fit for the job or company. That's not your fault, and you have choices.

3. **Is it really me?** *The external environment seems to be objectively fair and reasonable, yet you are still crippled with anxiety. Have you thought about getting some help? Generalized anxiety disorder is a very commonly diagnosed mental health issue—and easily treated over time. Don't be afraid to go there. There is no shame in admitting you need help. If you had kidney disease, you would treat it without a second thought. Why is mental health any different? And you will feel SO. MUCH. BETTER. Trust me. And you won't feel so alone, one of the most debilitating aspects of impostor syndrome.*

In the meantime, here is a framework to manage through the inevitable episodes of impostor syndrome when they hit. Not the chronic anxiety kind—but those times in your life when you are in a new role or leading for the first time and worry that you aren't measuring up. Instead of turning all of the fear and judgment and doubt inward and beating yourself up, think about it this way: It is part of good old-fashioned change management! We go through this throughout life; we deal with it all the time in business.

If you are running a team project to fix something, there are stages, right? First, it is hard. You struggle to define the problem and the solution. You debate and argue about it. There is uncertainty and stress. How can we define this, and get our arms around it? Then, you effectively get fluent about the problem and you can collectively, effectively start brainstorming solutions. At some point you think, "Good! We are heading in the right direction here—we've got this." At that point, it almost becomes fun: "We have defined it, solved it, now we communicate our work and take credit for it. Success!" You learn, grow, and conquer, then rinse and repeat. Now just think of yourself as this project! Of course it's hard and confusing in the beginning. Don't judge it. It's natural. Go with it. Give yourself some grace.

I think it is telling that when impostor syndrome hits, the inward focus of it can actually impact outward opportunities. Tara Sophia Mohr, in an August 2014 *Harvard Business Review* article, found that an average of 43 percent of applicants, when asked why they didn't apply for a job, stated that they thought they didn't meet the qualifications and they didn't want to waste their time. It also reported that almost twice as many women than men said that they didn't want to try and fail—and Mohr reports that there is some validity to that, referencing the Clayman Institute for Gender Research's claim: "There is, [in fact] some evidence to suggest that women's failures are remembered longer than men's."

Mohr continues: "People who weren't applying believed they needed the qualifications not to do the job well, but to be hired in the first place. They thought that the required qualifications were ... well, required." Potential applicants didn't consider that they could advocate for themselves as being qualified for the job, perhaps by creatively framing their past experiences. "What held them back from applying was not a mistaken perception about themselves, but a mistaken perception about the hiring process." Often, HR departments that craft the job listings do not have an accurate understanding of what is actually needed to complete the job. (Have you ever seen a job listing requiring y years of experience with a technology that has only existed for x years?) Others may be listing their "would be nice to have" traits under "requirements."

If we can overcome the urge not to even try—because, again, we are giving ourselves our own performance review before we've even started—think of the additional opportunities, additional learning environments, and the additional exposure to people and problems of the business world that await you!

Great Expectations

One of the consumer product companies I worked for had a standard Monday morning marketing meeting that even we finance dweebs got invited to—mostly so we would more easily approve their expenditures later, I'm sure. They were led by a guy who headed the marketing department, I'll call him Dan—a super talented, if a bit intense, individual. He would methodically review each of the product campaigns, its progress to date, messaging, and likelihood of success. I learned a great deal about marketing in these meetings, which I appreciated. I also noted that they were more casual and more interactive than our typical finance group meetings.

I have always been drawn to marketing types—the consumer insights and customer intimacy studies fascinate me. I sometimes wonder if I maybe should have gone that direction. At any rate, I don't think it's a coincidence that most of the friends I've made in the corporate world are marketing wonks.

So I really enjoyed these meetings and I became friendly with many of the attendees.

There came a time when the leader's executive assistant announced she was pregnant and talked to Dan about the timing of her maternity leave. Rumor had it that he had never had to deal with that before, and because she was so instrumental to him, he was quite put out at the prospect of losing her for several months.

A few weeks later, his favorite and best brand manager made the same announcement. It seemed the marketing department was overrun with pregnancies!

Somehow, those of us remaining, having heard about all of this, came up with a scheme we thought would be hilarious. We planned to all arrive at the next meeting "pregnant"—guys included. We all got fake pregnancy pillows and stuck them under our clothes for the meeting.

We waited with anxious anticipation for the inevitable howling that would occur.

Well, Dan walked in, looked around, and started the meeting. He didn't even notice! When someone prompted him and he clued in, we all stood up.

We thought we were hilarious, but apparently, Dan didn't. He looked at us, rested a beat, and then said, "Right, let's get on with the meeting now."

So we all sat there for another two hours, pregnancy pillows intact, and shuffled out of the room at the end. So anticlimactic!

14

It Sucks To Be a CFO

"It's shoot the messenger. The CFO often is the fall guy or the scapegoat for companies that don't make their numbers— the CFO ... has to tell people the bad news."

—John Challenger

ere is a recently reported statistic from Datarails based on SEC filings of the top 1,657 companies: The average tenure of a CFO is three years and one month, by far the lowest of any C-suite role. The common fate of a CFO, other than retirement, is either burnout, firing, or health issues. There are always situations where there is an urgent need for a CFO to drop in quickly—to either hold the seat while a search is done, or to bring specific skills into an unusual situation or challenge—like an IPO, or a cost-reduction mandate, or a merger.

Being an interim CFO was perfect for me. Although it didn't carry the professional recognition that other CFO roles did, I found it to be the perfect mixture between problem-solving, people management, strategy, tactical execution, and triage. It required parachuting into a situation, immediately assessing the issues, and coming up with a plan to survive and grow. The problems were urgent, so the environments were typically very supportive of transition. Decisions were rapid-fire, and action took precedence over process. I liked that. I also liked that once the problems were solved, it was time to move on. I had always found the more routine parts of being a CFO less engaging. For me, it was the perfect mix between having the support of partners within the CFO firm who understood and operated in the same environment, and being a C-suite executive independently trying to come up with the best alternatives for success for the company where I was interim CFO.

My roles usually lasted anywhere from eighteen months to three years. I was typically engaged either by the CEO or by the board itself, depending on the circumstances. I worked with smart people and fixed interesting problems. I got to experience different-sized companies, in different industries, and in a variety of ownership structures (public, private, private equity, venture). It was stimulating and fun—and the problem-solving side of me loved the challenge. And was there ever variety! Over the years I was in the C-suite for companies in technology, employee benefits, insurance, payroll processing, IT outsourcing, and foodservice.

I had crazy experiences, including being brought in after one CEO was arrested on embezzlement charges. (He is currently in prison.) I was informed that the DOJ had bugged my phone and my office, since the CEO was not yet in custody while awaiting trial and would wander the halls "chatting" with people. I had another where we stretched payables so much that our furniture was repossessed—on a day that we had investors coming in. We had to sit on the floor "Kum ba yah" style. I had yet another where I threw my back out the morning of a board meeting and had to call my kids' pediatrician for painkillers. To this day I remember nothing about that meeting, but apparently, I volunteered for all kinds of additional work! While these were entertaining, they were also stressful; parachuting in to fix things means you have to very quickly assess the situation with an objective eye. And I grew that muscle pretty well.

I did, over time, learn to ascertain things more quickly and discovered my own "tricks of the trade." For example, although I am not a smoker, I would go on "smoking" breaks with the executive assistants. I have found time and time again that they are undervalued and underappreciated, yet they usually sit out in the open and have a front-row seat to all that goes on. As such, they are in a perfect position to very quickly teach about the company. I would work hard to gain their trust (and never abused it) by promising that I would always tell them the truth, I would try my best to preserve their jobs, and I would keep what they told me confidential. They were so insightful and useful! I always made it my practice to treat them with a lot of respect. Just because they were in an assistant role, it didn't mean they weren't important or smart. They knew who the good and bad leaders were. They knew who the strong team players were and who were out for only themselves. And they were, honestly, a nice break in otherwise hectic and fast-paced days.

As an aside, at the Golden Globes in 2024, Ayo Edebiri won Best Supporting Actress for *The Bear*, and in her acceptance speech she said she wanted to thank "all of my agent's and manager's assistants, the people who answer my emails. Y'all are the real ones. Thank you for answering my crazy, crazy, emails," and she got applause. Right on!

Another "trick of the trade" was to get to know the board members and establish credibility and rapport right away. In many cases they become the decision-makers because it is not uncommon for the CEO to change out during a period of crisis. Working with the board provided the continuity needed for managing through change in the executive ranks and also created longer-lasting relationships that often transcended individual companies and could lead to future roles in other companies.

Over time, I came to recognize that no matter the size, industry, or ownership structure of a company, the problems usually stemmed from one of three areas:

1. A weak balance sheet that didn't provide the liquidity and working capital to support business downturns

2. Growth that occurred too quickly and ahead of proven success

3. Bad leadership

The latter was by far the most common and in several instances, I needed to go above the CEO's head to flag leadership issues. It was striking to me how many CEOs *were* the problem, the reason the company was in trouble, yet they couldn't see their own flaws. In several cases the CEO who hired me was terminated—and in several of those cases I ran the company while the board searched for a new leader. This always made starting a new CFO role a highly unpredictable experience. One day you show up and report to a CEO; shortly thereafter they are gone and there is a leadership void.

I remember the day I showed up at one job, an ambulance was parked in front of the building, and as I ascended the front steps, my new boss, the CEO, was carried out on a stretcher in the midst of a heart attack. Although we stayed in touch from afar while he worked through his health crisis, we never spent one day together in that office. And he never returned. He himself had been in an interim position from the private equity firm that funded the company. But, boy, did that accelerate the search for a new CEO.

Of course, there were challenges. HR issues were plentiful—the weirdest one being when I learned in one role that my executive assistant was a cross-dresser. She was so good at it, I never knew! But her work and attendance were pretty bad and so I told HR I wanted to let her go. My chief human resource officer said to me, "Well, you know 'she' is a 'he' right?" I had no idea! That made it more complicated for sure.

And of course, there were lots of layoffs—a very sad and difficult part of the turnaround business. I had to let a lot of people go. That never gets easier, but overhiring is a typical problem for troubled companies; they expand too quickly and drain cash. I actually received a thank-you note once from someone I had to terminate, telling me that she appreciated the dignity and empathy that I showed her in the process. Having had my own experiences with exits, it did teach me to appreciate the many emotions that come with an unexpected departure. Being and feeling out of control is no fun. I wish more senior executives had experience with and empathy for that.

Also, most of these companies were cash strapped and so I had limited staff and usually took on multiple roles. Over the years I had IT, legal, HR, and risk management reporting to me. I held the COO role more than once as well. I rarely had an executive assistant, so I learned to do a lot of my own administrative work. In addition, there was of course pressure to fix the business, and some boards and CEOs could handle that pressure better than others. I learned not to take it personally when I found myself shot for being the messenger of unwelcome news. And as time went on and I got better and more confident, I learned to think of myself as almost a doctor of sorts; I had the expertise that they needed and even if I was the person who communicated the diagnosis, I was also the healer and helper who prescribed the right medicine.

I also learned the "art" of saying no—which CFOs have to say a lot. It can strain relationships and cause people to be afraid to approach you and that is counterproductive. Some just outright hate you, blaming you for the layoffs and the day-to-day stresses and strains. You had to get comfortable with being disliked, feared, or some combination of the two. But I will say, it wasn't until I retired that I ever experienced people not returning phone calls. When you are the CFO, people *always* return your calls.

In difficult situations, I always tried to come up with an alternative to turn the conversation to a more positive and constructive conclusion. Instead of "no" *period*, I now always try to come up with a "no" *and* (as in "no, *and* what about this" or "no, *and* have we tried to do it another way?"). Building trust and turning negative conversations into positive problem-solving sessions were critical survival skills in successfully executing these turnaround roles. It was very satisfying work.

In my seven interim assignments, I never had a company fail. I learned a lot. I made good friends. And I gained some level of financial security—just in time for my boys to head to college! And thank goodness for that, because for years I struggled with saving and had to live paycheck to paycheck. I remember consulting a financial planner at one point when I was working my way up the finance ladder, and she casually told me that I was ten years behind and would never be able to afford to educate my kids. She must have gone to the same bedside-manner school that the doctor who delivered my first child did! Phew—it was a relief to finally have a meaningful nest egg—even if it was all earmarked for college tuition.

Although I loved it, that phase naturally came to a close when the CFO firm asked me to come inside and run the CFO practice from a thought-leadership and client-relationship perspective. I did that role for several years before retiring. It was a completely different role than that of a CFO—it was more people management because we had over three hundred CFOs in the practice at that time. In addition, I was able to step back and counsel others to make every engagement as successful as possible. I interacted directly with a number of clients to facilitate a good CFO experience for them—sometimes replacing CFOs to ensure a better fit, or changing out skill sets as the problems evolved.

Sometimes, it involved counseling the CFOs themselves when they encountered a thorny issue. My most memorable experience in that regard was with someone who had just given a pretty critical performance review to someone on their staff. She had been making a lot of mistakes and forgetting things. Apparently, he said to her, "It's like a piece of your brain is missing." Yes, a terrible thing to say in a performance review!—but she came back with, "It is—I had brain surgery last year." He came to me looking for the right words to go back to her with when he apologized!

While in that role, I hit the speaking circuit with a presentation I jokingly called, "It Sucks to Be a CFO"—the actual title was "CFOs Under Pressure: Achieving the Functional Imperative," which was an analytical (while still somewhat humorous) approach to understanding all of the stresses and changes that had occurred in the CFO world post-Enron and -Tyco. Various regulatory changes had wreaked havoc on the many responsibilities CFOs had to master in order to successfully do their jobs. The process side of the role had expanded to such an extent that CFOs found it hard to find time for the value-add parts of their jobs, and turnover rates were skyrocketing at the time.

The gist of it was that the extreme pressure was being driven by six specific factors: regulatory activity, financial market conditions, audit committee demands, the frustration of servicing data requests from all functional areas, staff support and management, and the lifestyle issues of long hours and inflexible schedules.

The perception of CFOs as unapproachable and rigid was also tackled. CFOs, like all of us, revert to their "comfort zone" characteristics under pressure, which in our case means becoming more skeptical, risk averse, detailed, analytical, and low on empathy. This doesn't help our cause and it would behoove us to learn (as I did) to overcome these tendencies and reach out, instead of shut down.

It was wildly popular and I was the keynote speaker at many finance conferences and CFO of the year award ceremonies. But for me it was also therapeutic because I was able to analyze and laugh at the many experiences I had had over the years. And perhaps it helped in a small way to let CFOs know that their expanded expectations, higher personal liability, and job stresses were real, and that there were ways to deal with that to make it better. I was very proud of that work, and I was not surprised to learn that the statistics have held up pretty well in today's CFO world since post-COVID, many things are changing again and stresses are high. *Fortune* magazine featured an article in 2024 titled "The Great CFO Turnover," which states that CFO turnover is 8.9 percent globally each year, outpacing both 2022 and 2023—in the US that's 163,000 CFOs. And a lot are opting out—retirements are up 15 percent year over year.

So I found that there is an endless demand for crisis CFOs, because we drop in so quickly to save the company going through long stretches without such a crucial role. But being in demand didn't change the fact that once I was in, the jobs were tough. And, in my very last crisis CFO role before I transitioned to run the CFO practice, I had my last toxic boss.

* * *

There are bosses who lie, try to take credit for your work, hit on you, or belittle you. I've had all of them. I have been through twenty-three direct bosses in my career. Out of those twenty-three, there were three really bad ones. And they all shared other qualities as well: They were combative, insecure, and critical. They didn't want to hear the truth, were narcissistic and duplicitous, were two-faced, had no EQ, and criticized my personality instead of my performance. And while their superiors thought they were great, they were all despised by those who were lower on the totem pole. They needed sycophants to constantly suck up to them. And their humor, if they had any, was mean.

One, and only one, of my interim CFO roles had shadows of my Pete and Tim experiences. I didn't notice it at first when I came in and assessed the issues and began to work with the CEO. The company was troubled—the top line was shrinking and the public company requirements for quarterly results were putting pressure on the team. The board was newly comprised and the chairman was a hedge-fund guy who was demanding and impatient. He also had a huge ego. They had just hired the CEO, who had industry experience but was fairly new in the CEO role. He was super smart, a bit of an introvert, but had the right mixture of financial savvy and marketing chops. His first action was to move the company from a major East Coast city to Chicago. I was hired a few months before the move and for the first few months worked in the East Coast office. Things started out OK.

I found our Chicago office space and built an entirely new finance team for the new location. I also counseled out the local finance team and shut down the East Coast office. Once in the Midwest, we re-IPOed the company to raise additional capital, went on a road show to sell the deal, and started to focus on growth again. I built relationships with the investors. I produced a ton of extra materials requested by the board, and I even led a restatement of the prior year financials—without negatively impacting the stock—to correct for some incorrect accounting treatment which had occurred prior to my arrival. This being my eighth CFO role, I really knew what I was doing by this time. In all honesty, I would give myself an A for what I accomplished and for my part in the results that we had started to produce.

Yet something was off. I never felt like I was part of a team and I had an uncomfortable relationship with the chairman. He was on-site every other week—very odd and not typical or helpful. He asked for a lot of ancillary requests that took time and produced little value. He tended to lecture, not discuss. However, he and the CEO had a very close relationship. Too close, in my opinion. They referred to themselves as "brothers" and would disappear for lunches or store visits without including others. I observed that some of my peers sucked up to them a lot, fulfilling that sycophant role. That wasn't my style, so I just put my head down and did my work.

But the discomfort was always there. We initiated a stock offering about a year after I started, and during that launch, the three of us went on the road to market the deal. While on the road show, they were very rude—sharing a lot of private jokes, going to dinner without me, and discussing other people's compensation and performance disparagingly in front of me. I was miserable on that trip and became very concerned about my own future with the company. If they talked that way about everyone else, it was clear to me that they'd do the same to me. So I started to talk to my CFO boss about it and I started to think about how to work in such a toxic environment and still preserve my sanity.

It all came to a head when I saw that the chairman was turning in excessive expenses that we should not be reimbursing. The first few times, I corrected the amounts and put the rest through for reimbursement. But the amounts kept growing. I finally decided that I needed to tell the CEO, and so I went into his office, showed him several examples, and told him that I thought it was a problem but that I was not sure the best way to handle it. "I'll take care of it," he said. "You did the right thing." The following day, a Friday, I went to an afternoon Cubs game with our audit partner. The following Monday morning at nine a.m., the CEO fired me. I was not a good "cultural" fit, he said—without providing any examples. When I asked about my performance, he said he had no suggestions for improvement. He and the chairman just thought it was time for a change.

Although I can't ever factually connect the dots, I will always believe that my going to the CEO about the chairman (his "brother") cost me my job. He repeatedly referred to the chairman being part of the decision-making process over the weekend. Not only did they fire me, they insisted that I be escorted out of the building, an unnecessary humiliation, and they put out a press release with a headline saying that they were "strengthening the finance department." It was surprising and disturbing and embarrassing. But it was also not my first rodeo.

Thank God my CFO partners completely supported me, and I was thankful that I had wanted to have support behind me as one of my earlier job tenets—I did not feel the isolation that I had with Tim or Pete. In fact it was at that point that I was promoted internally at that firm and brought inside to lead the CFO practice. I guess they figured by then I had seen it all—the good, the bad, and the ugly—and so I could counsel others through the ups and downs of the corporate world.

In some ways this one didn't sting as much—I had grown a thicker skin and had a bit of a "you win some, you lose some" mentality. I was also much more financially secure and had had enough success behind me so that my confidence honestly wasn't shaken. But in some ways, it was worse because I was mad . . . so mad. I knew beyond a shadow of a doubt that my performance was stellar. I did not deserve what happened and I was truthfully somewhat concerned about my professional reputation. I was on two public company boards at this point and needed to make awkward phone calls to each of them to explain what had happened. That was not fun. But I had so many wins under my belt by that point that, despite the momentary brou-haha, I very quickly emerged unscathed and went on to really enjoy leading the CFO practice for several years before retiring. It seems things happen for a reason—there was a high level of turnover at that company subsequently, and eventually it went out of business. And I cashed out a few points below the all-time stock high, while later it diminished to become a penny stock.

And, as usually happens with bad leaders, both the CEO and the chairman not only eventually flamed out and left the company (with the stock in the toilet), but they apparently had some sort of personal falling-out and ended up completely estranged. Yet, there were still lessons to be learned. They fired a few other high performers after me and left a lot of scar tissue for those others. They had a cavalier disregard for people's feelings and efforts. There are far more gentle and respectful ways to exit people from their roles without the crass treatment and shady motives. And perhaps I could have come up with a more creative way to deal with the issues I faced, but for the life of me, I still can't figure out what that might have been. Sometimes life is just unfair. Sometimes, even when you should win, you lose. Or, as Dirk put it, quoting the wisdom of Dire Straits: "Sometimes you're the windshield and sometimes you're the fly."

Gender Bender

You can't make this stuff up. One of my favorite CFO roles was for a start-up company in the employee benefits area. We struggled but grew consistently, eventually selling the company to a bigger player in the field. In this case, the crazy story has nothing to do with the business itself and everything to do with people's personal lives playing out in the office.

We had a management team that was small but complete. It included, among others, a head of HR (an African American woman over forty—therefore part of what is called a "protected class") and a head of operations (a white man). It all started when the head of ops (I'll call him Patrick) came to the CEO and complained that he was being sexually harassed by the head of HR (I'll call her Sarah). Sarah apparently had a crush on him (according to Patrick) and continually followed him home and parked outside of his house.

Since it was the head of HR that we were talking about here, we obviously could not involve her. So I was brought in to work with the CEO to figure out what to do. While my boss and I had our doubts about what might or might not have been going on, we clearly needed to do some investigation. And we needed to be fair and unbiased, especially given the age and race considerations. But before we could even get a game plan together to start investigating, Patrick asked for a meeting with both of us and revealed even more. The reason he was so upset about the harassment, he told us, was because it upset his wife. And he was concerned about upsetting his wife because he was in the process of filing for divorce from her and he didn't want her thinking that the divorce was caused by Sarah, who was visibly parking outside of his house every night. It might complicate the proceedings.

Believe me, we did not ask him why he was getting divorced—yet he felt he needed to share. Patrick then told us that he was in the process of starting a gender transition—and he no longer wanted to be married to his wife because he was in love with another woman, who was a lesbian. He was transitioning so that he could be with the woman he loved.

Well. It took my boss and me some time to wrap our heads around all of this.

At the end of the day, we decided together that all of the noise around Patrick's divorce really had nothing to do with the business and we needed to respect his privacy. However, the accusations against the head of HR were well within our purview, so my boss and I confronted her. We had a plan but as soon as we were in the room with her, my boss decided not to confront her directly and to go off-script. Instead, he "posed a hypothetical" to her while I watched, aghast … this was not the plan. But he launched into asking her for "advice" about the "fact" that he was in love with someone in the company and found himself following her home every night. "I'm pretty sure this is bad, right? I mean, I shouldn't be doing this," he said. "I'd probably lose my job. I'm sure." Sarah got quieter and quieter while he laid out exactly what she had been doing without ever accusing her. Eventually he stopped; I had to overcome my shock, since he had embellished quite a bit, and I realized he was kind of enjoying this little charade.

As he wrapped up and the silence lingered, Sarah looked down. "OK," she said, finally looking up, "I quit—I'll be out by the end of the day." So ended one of the most bizarre human resources experiences I have ever had—or even heard about.

But what makes me laugh to this day is the aftermath when we informed Patrick that it had been handled and wished him luck with his remaining personal circumstances. He became thoughtful at the end of that conversation and pondered out loud, "I wonder if people will still like me as a woman?"

My boss—without missing a beat—responded, "Patrick, they don't like you now!"

15

Change

"I am here to tell you that if you ever encounter a dip in your life, pay no attention to the voice inside of you that judges you, that is negative, that fosters further anxiety . . . just follow your curiosities."

—Isabella Rossellini

Yes, obviously unexpected change is a part of life. We all learned that at a very early age, when our mothers forced us out of the house and into school. When we had to head off to college. When we didn't get into the college of our choice. When our first love left us. No one hits adulthood without some level of experience with change. And I would also argue change is actually productive and healthy. It is what creates growth opportunities. But change usually reveals its value in retrospect. In real time, it can really suck, especially if it is unwanted, unwelcome, and shakes your foundation to its very core. I'm talking about professional change. The kind that happens *to* you—comes at you gradually, yet still has draconian implications.

Even "lower-level" traumas—upheavals that don't involve illness, death, or divorce—can impact your entire life, not just your work life. They can have lasting impacts on friendships, résumés, and self-esteem. They can fundamentally shake your belief in a fair and just meritocracy. They can reveal bad behavior—or more likely, bad leadership. And you are in a victim role with no say over what is happening and how you "got here."

As a crisis CFO, I dropped into many situations rife with chaos, anarchy, fear, panic, and confusion. I have sorted them out, endeavored to decode them and then bring some level of stability and sanity to the situation. There is a process to do that—but that is not where I want to focus right now. I want to talk about what it feels like to find yourself in a bad situation—like I have earlier in my career as a victim and later in my career as a fixer. I want to capture the buildup, the acceleration, and ultimately, the insanity that can envelop a corporate culture. And I want to provide advice about how to live through it.

First, let us just assert that the world in these last nine years has itself provided a rich canvas of chaos for all of us as a society to weather—so we have a starting point. We have all started to build this muscle. When Trump upended the 2016 election to shock the country and the world from the expected result—it started. He then led an administration filled with surprise entrances and exits, shifted international balances, and created a nonstop news cycle of "What is happening now?" Sure—a lot of that connected with a lot of people who cheered on the challenge to the status quo. But the pace and velocity of change was accelerated instantaneously.

Then came COVID. Again—out of the blue, some very foundational parts of our day-to-day existence were challenged. We couldn't socialize in person; we couldn't travel; we couldn't smile because our faces were covered with masks. Hell, we couldn't even go to the grocery store in a "normal" way. And the leadership of the country couldn't tell us in a unified voice what was going on, what caused it, when it was going to get better, and how to survive it. Contradictory advice was all over the airwaves. And it lasted for years. We adapted. We will again.

We're again in a state of flux, only a few months into Trump's second term as of this book's release, as executive orders and lawsuits and threats of tariffs fly back and forth, leaving governmental employees and the private sector in a state of whiplash. Sadly, foreign aid and our ability to be a country for safe refuge may be permanently impacted. I am a trustee for Save the Children, and the impact of the new cutbacks are devastating to the help and aid that we pride ourselves on providing worldwide to children in crisis. So many will die.

While it's impossible to predict what all this turmoil will cause, I cannot tell you how representative all of that is to a company in crisis. Early warnings are ignored or explained away; denial takes over; the velocity of change and the inadequacy of fact-based reporting skyrockets. And, yes, often different leaders convey wildly different takes on the situation. Your ability to feel invisible, unempowered, and threatened is heightened. So let's step into a company where you find yourself working. Maybe you've been there for a while; you are used to the protocols and processes in play. Then you slowly notice work isn't the same place anymore. Things have started to "feel" different. Is it you? Is it something in some other part of your life pulling at you? Or are you seeing the early signs of trouble—not in your life yet—but around you?

Here are the early warnings that change is afoot:

- There are a lot of closed doors and mysterious meetings.

- The rumor mill suddenly picks up with conspiracy theories and gossip.

- Budget cuts are made and expenses are suddenly scrutinized or denied.

- Approval processes—even if ultimately successful—take longer and longer.

- Travel is cut.

- Hiring is frozen; raises are delayed.

- Turnover increases—in particular, high-potential performers suddenly jump ship.

- Corporate communication shifts—often, sadly, there is less of it; what does occur starts reflecting a new vocabulary.

- Top executive jobs are rotated to new people, new faces.

- Focus moves quickly to driving the top line, although results are largely driven by cutting costs.

It is important to see these in their totality. At lower levels, these often won't be as obvious. And one or two of these does not always indicate trouble—but get to four or more of these? I'd bet money that things are heading south and you'd better prepare yourself. How do you do that? The first step is just to accept and internalize the fact that change is afoot. Depending on how you feel about your company and your role, this may involve some shock, some sadness, some fear, and maybe even some grieving. Give yourself a bit of time to adjust; these things don't come crashing down overnight.

Next, baldly assess your level of commitment to this institution. What is your loyalty level? If it's low, then start looking around. This is not a time for people-pleasing; throw your impostor syndrome to the side. Action is required! And when you do start looking around, do not throw your current company under the bus. Come up with justifiable reasons why you want to change jobs without pointing fingers or burning bridges. That's important; life is long and things have a way of coming around. Plus, the person you are interviewing with may get turned off—vengeance is not attractive and says volumes about your character.

But let's say that you want to stay. There could be many reasons for this. First—believe me—you learn *a lot* in crisis situations. It is difficult and draining but it can really strengthen your leadership abilities. You may also find, like I did, that regardless of the specific circumstances, the challenges of troubled companies kind of turn you on. For me, it turned into a new career. But it is surely not for everyone, and assessing your ability to contribute and shine while in the midst of profound change is also important to think about. Also, you may choose to do it to preserve relationships, in the hopes that on the other side, people you have stood with will present you with new opportunities. When I was a crisis CFO, I had a terrific group of people whom I often took from job to job with me because I knew they were unflappable and dependable. Finally, you may need to stay out of financial necessity or to preserve an arrangement that you have negotiated that you don't believe you can replicate elsewhere. All are good reasons.

As I said at the beginning of this, change creates opportunity, but only if you seize it. The most important thing you can do, if you've made a firm decision to stay, is to raise your hand and step into the fray. Merely hiding in the hopes of surviving is not a good strategy. Management will really appreciate the outreach; typically they themselves are floundering. When so many are hiding or jumping ship a person can really stand out by saying, "I want to be part of the solution; what can I do to help?" I would be shocked if they didn't take you up on it—and if your profile doesn't rise beneficially!

Leaning heavily on a document created for one of my current boards, here is a list of attributes that are valued in a turnaround setting; evaluate yourself against them. See if you:

- Can think and move quickly

- Proactively build partnerships internally and externally

- Develop associates and teams who are better than you

- Use radical "just-in-time" prioritization

- Are emotionally intelligent

- Speak up

- Can zoom in **and** zoom out

- Thrive while operating "in the gray"

- Embrace failure as part of the learning process

- Move fast

- Don't take things personally, and don't dwell on things

- Are comfortable being uncomfortable

- Have grit

- Understand the difference between wisdom and knowledge

- Ask "What would it take?" instead of saying "Here's why we can't."

- Are self-aware

If you choose to do a pro and con analysis of staying versus leaving, consider these factors:

If you leave, you are exposed to a new opportunity (people, industry, role). There could be wonderful things that come out of that, but it is a gamble. You may make more money. You may avoid the trauma and stress of being with a company undergoing a transformation. You may also burn bridges and leave elements of your current job unfinished—thereby unable to truly claim accomplishment and victory in the future.

If you stay, brace yourself for long hours, lots of uncertainty, and a volatile work environment. Expect stress levels and emotionalism in the workplace to rachet up. But also look at the skills that you will learn that you will take with you forever. These include the ability to prioritize, effective decision-making on limited information under time pressure, important communication techniques to inform, motivate, and reward people, contacts for the future, and—importantly—perspective.

I will say that my ability to stay calm in a crisis—even as a CFO, even as a single mom—was honed by appreciating the fact that no matter how bad corporate upheaval can be, it is *not* a level I trauma, like illness, dislocation, or divorce. There are people going through so much more hardship. It taught me gratitude, as funny as that may sound. But all of this assumes there is a beginning, a middle, and a conclusion to a specific corporate turnaround or crisis.

But what if things are permanently changing? The world as we know has and will continue to absorb much change in these past few years; some of it likely to be permanent. The advance of AI, in particular, along with accelerating technological improvements, will forever change the way business is done, from both a promising perspective (efficiencies and creative advances) as well as a defensive point of view (cybersecurity risks). In addition, the world around us is shifting at an alarming pace. Geopolitical alliances are shifting; rightwing conservatism and nationalism are on the rise, and the Middle East has become alarmingly unstable. Here in the US, at the beginning of the second Trump term, there lies the possibility for draconian border-control policies and significant trade tariffs. All of these are impacting business today and well into the future.

But to my mind, nothing is as complicated for our daily work life than the transformation which has occurred post-COVID to drive the work-from-home (WFH) movement. What started out of necessity has been wildly embraced by some and lamented by others. It has benefited a significant portion of the working population, specifically moms, people who had long commutes, people with disabilities, and those who can do their job independently. All without requiring a lot of meetings or interaction. But it is complicated.

To be honest, I straddle both sides of this issue. Had I had the ability to work from home when my kids were little, it would have been transformative. Just the ability to drop off and pick up the kids, throw a load of laundry in, or start dinner during the day, while still being highly productive, would have been a game changer. And I completely embrace the trust that this implies; let us, finally, treat people as responsible adults and believe that they (we!) will live up to our responsibilities. It also balances out the power structure that heretofore was stacked heavily toward favoring men with a support system around them, which allowed them to focus exclusively on their jobs (and golf games), while so many others were torn in so many competing directions. It simplifies a lot. It reduces commuting time, wasted meeting time, and water-cooler gossip time.

But it also eliminates the ability to build a culture—and as much as this generation disdains that idea, I have experienced both the positive and negative impacts that culture can have. What I have not experienced—and I wonder about—is the inability to build a culture. How do you rally people around a corporate mission? How do you create a brand that stands for something? That takes interaction;

it takes more well-rounded experience of each other than continual Zoom meetings. I believe it is important to have multilevel, multifunctional familiarity, interaction, respect, and problem-solving. I worry that the younger generation doesn't have a chance to watch, to learn, to grow, to be mentored as effectively as prior generations have had. I don't know what that will do to impact future leaders.

I have this conversation frequently with my sons' significant others—all in the work world, some struggling with balancing motherhood with career ambitions. They love the work-from-home option. They feel resentful when the recent trend of back-to-office mandates threatens their freedom. I get that. I really do. But I can't help but wonder: How can you be an agent for change from the outside? Can you have as meaningful a career—over the long term—from your kitchen? Can you have as much impact?

I don't know the answer. But I worry about it. I have had enough leadership experience to know that a team does not come together organically very often when all of its members are remote from each other. It is a three-dimensional version of a long-distance relationship—with all of the challenges that brings.

Each of these types and facets of change brings unique challenges, yet all require a similar playbook: observe, assess, decide, act. To do that, have a clear sense of who you are, what you bring, what your nonnegotiables are, and what trade-offs you are willing to make. Actions taken today may have deep implications for tomorrow. So don't be motivated by fear or by doing what other people want you to do. This is the time, if you haven't already, to discover (or rediscover) agency!

Dress for Success

In one of my CFO roles, I had an executive assistant who was awesome. Her name was Jan. She was so good that we gave her several additional roles, one of which was to be the general receptionist, greeting visitors when they came through the door. She was a very friendly person, so this made a lot of sense.

Jan had a weight problem—a very significant one that impacted her life from both a health and a social perspective. She decided to get surgery to deal with it.

The surgery was smashingly successful and it was fun over the next six months or so to see her lose over one hundred pounds. She had a new lease on life! She was upbeat and energetic and oh-so-proud of herself, as she had every right to be.

The problem started when we collectively began noticing that she was dressing very provocatively. Low-cut tops, very short skirts, massive amounts of jewelry. The CEO called me into his office to talk about it. He was uncomfortable, he said, given that she was in such a public position. He wondered what our guests would think.

"But I, as a man, can't really have this conversation with her comfortably," he said. "I need for you to have it—besides, she reports to you anyway, so it makes sense."

"Do you think it's going to be easy for me to have it?" I asked. It's a weird and awkward conversation for anyone to have!

So I stewed about it and I planned what I would say and how I would say it—I worried about it and I dreaded it.

Eventually I decided it was time, so I called Jan into my office and I gingerly told her that there was some concern about her wardrobe choices—that we were proud of her and her weight loss but that in the office, we needed a little more conservatism.

"Then I'll quit," said Jan.

I thought she was angry. I told her we didn't want her to quit and it wasn't meant to be so offensive that she'd go **that** far. She started laughing. "Cindie," she said, "I'm not mad. I understand. I just don't want to give this up. I have waited my whole life to dress like a slut and I am loving every minute of it—if the office can't deal with it, then I'll leave. But I plan to dress sluttier and sluttier!"

16

The Energy of Money

"Money often costs too much."

—Ralph Waldo Emerson

Being a CFO naturally means that you deal with money in all ways, shapes, and forms all day long. And you don't just deal with the actual handling of money, you deal with the *idea* of money constantly: where to spend it, whether or not to spend it, repercussions of spending it, repercussions of *not* spending it, etc. And so, most people think of a CFO's role as making those decisions—and helping other people to make them—in an objective, logical way. Right?

Wrong.

Sitting in the chair where people at all levels within an organization come to talk about money essentially gives you a front-row seat to the psychology of money. And money has a lot of power over people—in all kinds of ways. And so the privilege of that role is that it demystifies money and takes away a lot of its power—for the CFO, not necessarily for anyone else.

Money represents many different things to many different people. And the psychology of it is wrapped up in childhood stuff, practical stuff, self-image stuff, and identity stuff. If you stop and consider that "money" is just letters and symbols printed on paper, created by man simply as a medium for commerce to be effective and efficient, it seems crazy to watch all of the power that people give it. I had two close personal friends who both lived in my neighborhood when I was raising my kids. They could not have been more different on this front. One made a lot of money and spent even more. Approaching retirement, she had no savings, and really didn't seem to worry about that very much. The other made less money—but did fine—and had a hard time parting with a dime. She constantly pared down household bills and reduced services so that she could survive on less. Both asked me, at different points, to help them—neither listened to a word I said but went right back to their inherent ways. This stuff runs deep.

It is interesting to me that money brings out mostly negative emotions in people. Of course, for many the idea of money is tied up with the feeling of lack. And lack is fear based. Lack makes you want things—in some cases things that you might not otherwise want. Compare it to a diet. You may not want, or even think about, an ice cream sundae. But go on a diet and see a picture of one and the first thing you think is "I can't have that" and the second thing you think is "Now I want one." Lack brings up issues that can be complicated: It can trigger self-esteem and self-worth insecurities. On the other hand—like my one friend who volunteers for "lack," it can bring feelings of empowerment ("Look how little I can live on!")—but, like an anorexic, too much of that can be bad too. Either way, it's playing a major role in your day-to-day life.

Fear is a big element in the equation of money for a lot of people. "Money" equals "safety." And while there is no denying that money provides comfort, options, and convenience, it is a stretch to say that it and it alone provides safety. Money won't help you if you have an abusive partner. Money won't help you in a refugee camp. Money doesn't fix your health, your relationships, your racism or sexism or war. It truly has some power ... but limited power. Any power that it has, *you give it*.

Money can also bring up feelings of competitiveness—how much are you making compared to someone else and how does that make you feel? Are you OK with it? Are you angry about it? Does it make you willing to work harder to make more? Does it make you feel victimized and marginalized because "the man" decided your job was worth less than someone else's? Think about the extension of those feelings into government policy decisions. How does a society feel about "entitling" people for help with basic needs and services? Does everyone have a right to those, or should people "pull themselves up by their bootstraps" to better their own circumstances? And think about the inequities that a capitalist society produces based on simple market economics. Rock stars and sports stars can make hundreds of millions of dollars while teachers and nurses barely survive. Objectively speaking—who adds more to society?

Why do people feel so good when they get something for nothing? Why is there no shame in taking something that doesn't belong to you, or relishing finding someone else's loss? Recently I asked for cash back while checking out of the grocery store in the self-checkout area. I was distracted . . . on the phone and in the midst of a crazy day. I asked for forty dollars over my total but realized when I got to the car that I'd forgotten to grab the cash from the machine. In the three or four minutes it took for me to go back into the store, the cash was gone. No one had turned it in either. For forty dollars, it was no more than an annoyance (mostly at myself), but it says something about human nature that someone grabbed it and took it so quickly.

In some ways, "money" equals "love." We have some weird societal norms around it. I worked with a Norwegian guy once who mentioned this to me, what he called "the sexual transaction of money" in the USA. Huh? In Norway, he said, when people date, they each pay their own way. If they want to be together, they are together and it is separate from money. In the US, he said, women seem to expect the man to pay for her, but in return the man then has some (invalid) expectation of a "thank you," if you get my drift.

There are a lot of trust issues around money. Don't lend money to a friend; don't do business with family members; have a prenup before you get married. All of these adages are around the idea that you need to protect yourself because people can't be trusted to act appropriately or ethically if money is involved. How many families end up in court battling over estates and wills? How many divorcing couples spend months, if not years, arguing over the division of assets—sometimes quite illogically. I know a woman who will inherit a good bit of money soon—but it didn't stop her (or her lawyer) from going after her soon-to-be ex-husband mercilessly to try to get more and more from him—just because she felt he owed her that. That's a power play over a practical play.

Then there is the "gaming" of money—gambling, lottery tickets, sports betting—winning and losing, feeling good and feeling bad, "getting" versus "giving" . . . all wrapped up in money.

So when I say it's complicated, well, it's complicated! Simply explaining it logically to someone rarely works because people hold on to their beliefs and programming about money the way they do their most deeply held beliefs about life, religion, politics. I learned this the hard way. For some friends and family members, I have literally spent days building models, sending articles, researching websites, interviewing financial planners, and creating entire life plans for them to help get them out of trouble. And I felt used and angry when they couldn't find the time to even read half of what I sent. But then I realized they don't really want the help. They know they have a problem and they want it solved easily and painlessly—without actually suffering at all. They feel better simply because they asked for help, but they don't really want to do the hard work involved to change. It is like any other addiction (and, yes, people can be addicted to money). To quote Henry Cloud, "We change our behavior when the pain of staying the same becomes greater than the pain of changing. Consequences give us the pain that motivates us to change." I learned to set boundaries around what I will and what I won't do for people and I have gotten savvier at assessing their real intentions before doing the work. It is not my job, even for people I love, to participate in poor decision-making.

What are *my* thoughts and approaches about money? Like anyone else, I am sure that they are influenced by my personal experiences and worldviews. I grew up very comfortably—I never experienced hunger and I had my education provided for. That makes a difference. But I also lived paycheck to paycheck for decades as a single mom and so I know the struggle firsthand. We did not take vacations. My kids did not have the newest shoes or the best computers. Later in life I remarried, and coincident to that, I did quite well with my company equity grants as a director as well as in my personal investments (thank you, Kyle!).

From a variety of perspectives and in living and learning, observing and teaching, and of course, in dealing with the dollars day in and day out for struggling companies, here is my personal approach to money:

I believe there is a spiritual energy to money and that you can influence that through your beliefs and actions. If you feel abundance and you truly believe that you work hard, live with integrity, and that life is fair in the long run, money problems tend to work themselves out. Not every day in every way—but in the long haul. The principle of manifestation is the following: the practice of using intention, belief, and focused thought to bring something into reality. It is often linked to the law of attraction, which states that like attracts like and that our thoughts and emotions can shape our experiences.

Money has a particular velocity. Adam Smith, centuries ago, came up with the concept of the multiplier effect of currency. You hand one dollar to a clerk at McDonald's, that dollar goes into a bank deposit at the end of the day, that bank lends that dollar to a business to help it grow, that business spends that dollar to buy more inventory, the vendor that sells that inventory uses that dollar to make his payroll. And so it goes on. Next Generation Personal Finance estimates that 110 people touch a dollar bill in a year. And if you believe in the spiritual principle of manifestation, then you can believe and set your intention that some of that velocity should and will come your way.

How does one do that? I think positively that money will be there and that it will be enough (don't get greedy!) when I need it. I think positively all the time about it. But conversely, I do not think about it all the time. It is a small part of my life in terms of meaning. I don't hoard it—I give freely, from large donations to causes I believe in to tiny gestures (tipping well for good service). I get into the flow of the velocity of money and a) believe that I deserve some of it and b) pledge that I will be a good steward of it—using it wisely and unselfishly and for the greater good. I do this both professionally and personally.

I realize that to some, this may seem ethereal and amorphous. I am not trying to convince anyone anymore about what they should or shouldn't believe. I just know what I believe and that it has always worked for me. Intention is everything—as it so often is for so many things.

No Thanks

My very first turnaround CFO role was for a small public telecommunications company that used 4G technology (brand new at the time) to improve cell phone transmissions. The CEO interviewed me and then communicated to my boss at the CFO firm that he wanted to hire me. Arrangements were made and I started immediately. The compensation arrangement for that "dual-employment" situation was that I would be a full-fledged officer of the company—fully on the company's payroll. But once negotiated and agreed to, I would receive five-sixths of that amount and the CFO firm would receive one-sixth, paid as a vendor. All elements of the compensation, including equity grants and bonuses, were contractually agreed to upfront.

The CEO was a "science" guy and was deeply engaged in the product development aspect of the business. Clearly, he didn't pay much attention to the financial end of things, as I learned when I put together their first-ever cash flow analysis in my first week and quickly realized that the company had less than two months of cash available. How could this possibly happen? I quickly alerted the CEO and told him I planned to assemble a board meeting to communicate the emergency situation. He did not balk at that idea, but neither did he seem anywhere near as alarmed as one would have thought.

Our board was primarily composed of the private equity representatives who had originally seeded the business as a start-up. We connected on a telephonic board call and I communicated the dire financial situation facing us.

They were shocked. They were also, understandably, very upset with the CEO. Things quickly deteriorated between the two sides. They injected some fresh cash into the business (under fairly draconian terms) to allow us to continue operating, and they fired the CEO. They asked me to act as interim COO while they searched for a new CEO. For several months I did just that.

Fortunately, at that time the dot-com bubble occurred and for the next year or so, our stock was carried skyward on the coattails of internet stocks. I believe we went from under five dollars to something in the fifty-dollar range. The investors were ecstatic and cashed out a large portion of their investment at a hefty profit. They made tens of millions. They also eventually hired a new CEO. A nice enough guy, I didn't think he was anything special—but I was relieved to be back acting as "only" the CFO.

Over my tenure as interim COO, we had rescued our relationships with vendors, added to our marketing team and built brand awareness, and repaired our investor relations credibility. There were also tough times—layoffs that needed to occur and a lot of uncertainty with no CEO in place. To add to that, the old CEO had sued for wrongful termination and so we were embroiled in an ugly lawsuit for the remainder of my time in the role. It was a lot to juggle and I was constantly on the phone seven days a week with the private equity guys.

I considered my performance a real success from a CFO perspective. I had literally saved the company, rightsized the spending, worked closely with analysts and investors while the stock appreciated, and held down the COO role for months.

At the end of the first year, it was time to pay bonuses. The board approved the payment via email. Mine was, as I mentioned, contractually agreed to when I had joined, and so there was no discretion involved. I authorized the firmwide payouts based on the metrics all had agreed upon. I didn't think much about it because at that point, the equity I had been granted was worth several million dollars and was materially more meaningful to me. We presented the occurrence of the bonus payments at the next board meeting.

As was usual, at the end of the meeting management was excused while the board went into executive session. Something seemed off because they lingered in the boardroom much longer than usual. Eventually a more-junior private equity guy came out and pulled me aside.

"There is a problem with your bonus," he said. "You had no authority to pay yourself; it's an ethical issue and we have opened up a formal investigation into it."

Huh?

"What are you talking about?" I asked. "It's in my contract, and I was authorized to approve all of them." I was stunned and, frankly, offended. This was black and white and it was nonsensical to me that **this** is what they were focused on at that point. By the way, this was not a huge bonus either ... it just wasn't that meaningful and if they had a question about it, they could have asked me—or my CFO firm—for clarification. But to initiate a "formal" ethics investigation? **Come on.**

Ultimately, it became a tempest in a teapot—my boss at the CFO firm was livid and completely backed me up. I think he was madder than I was! And this completely validated why I had as one of my nonnegotiables never being hung out to dry alone again. They fought the battle for me and essentially told the private equity guys to go pound sand.

I was allowed to keep my bonus, but my CFO firm boss pulled me out of there immediately. Such an abrupt ending bothered me, but as I was to learn, a lot of crazy stuff happens not only in the turnaround world but also in the private equity world.

It felt unfair and a little sad to me. But it didn't feel like a failure, nor did I beat myself up about it. I left with a box of my stuff in hand, alone, walking out to the parking lot with no fanfare whatsoever. No one ever thanked me. No one even said good-bye.

I went on to my next CFO role almost immediately, which turned out to be a great placement and one that I enjoyed immensely and was where I met one of my favorite bosses ever—who I would work for multiple times in the coming years. In the meantime, the dot-com bubble burst, and by the time I was able to sell my stock, the value of it had fallen almost all the way back to where it had started. My millions of dollars' worth of stock ended up netting me about $60,000 after tax because I was precluded from selling any stock for six months based on the fact that I had been an officer and my trades would be publicly reported. To add insult to injury, I was the key witness in the lawsuit that involved the prior CEO. For several years I had numerous interactions with and depositions scheduled with the private equity guys who had questioned my ethics. Ridiculously, at one point while I was waiting in a conference room with the senior private equity guy before yet another deposition, he actually asked me why I left. I told him about the investigation. He knew nothing about it! And he told me I was the best CFO they'd ever had. **Sheesh.**

Finally, they ultimately settled the lawsuit with the ex-CEO and I could put my relationship with them in the rearview mirror.

17

Board Games

"In a world of well-defined problems, directors are required to exercise influence over volatility, manage uncertainty, simplify complexity, and resolve ambiguity in the 21st-century digital environment."

—Pearl Zhu

Recently, I was on a flight seated next to a lovely (if a little too chatty for my taste) woman who explained to me that she owns AirBnBs in Hawaii. She showed me pictures, she talked about the frustrations, and she tried mightily to cajole me into renting one of them; I didn't. But at the end of the flight, as we were landing, she said to me, "Can you help me get on a board?" This is but one example of a question I get frequently—from people both qualified to be on a board and not (like the AirBnB gal). It seems to be the in-vogue career destination for many who think that the role is a) lucrative, b) cushy, and c) easy. The gap between perception and reality is wide.

The boardroom isn't a place that is inherently comfortable for most people. It is rarified air, for sure. But it is also, like any other group dynamic, filled with personalities, competitiveness, and complexity. For those who need a primer, here are the basics: A public company board of directors is elected by, and represents, the shareholders of the company. As such, the responsibility is most directly to the interests of those who hold the stock—which doesn't necessarily mean that there isn't some level of responsibility to other constituencies, like employees and regulatory bodies, but primarily, the creation of share-holder value is the mandate.

The two most important things that a board does is to hire and evaluate the CEO, and to participate in and ultimately approve management's strategy for the business. A board is composed of anywhere from seven to twelve "independent" directors—meaning they have no other relationship with the company that would compromise their ability to think clearly and be unbiased in their decision-making—and the CEO, who is an "employee-director," and therefore not considered independent. Historically, the CEO was usually the chairman of the board, but these days that practice is frowned upon and best practice is to have a separate chairman and CEO.

There are also committees of the board, where a lot of the actual work gets done. The board has a regular cadence of quarterly meetings—usually two-to-three days long. The three standing committees are:

- **Audit**—responsible for the integrity of the financial statements and risk management)

- **Compensation**—responsible for CEO and C-suite executive compensation decisions

- **Nominating and Governance**—responsible for board composition, including recruiting new directors, and adherence to high principles of corporate governance like approving the bylaws, the committee charters, and the code of ethics for the company

Like anything else, there are pluses and minuses to being a public company director. Let's start with the pluses. Intellectually, the role is very fun and challenging. The board only deals with the most complex and consequential decisions facing the CEO and therefore the company. It is stimulating to engage in discussion and debate with a room full of super smart, super experienced executives (both management and board) to get to a collective point of view and decision on all kinds of business topics. And speaking of those smart people . . .

everyone in the room has a depth of experience—in both business and life—that renders them thoughtful, articulate, and insightful.

I believe that the reason most directors are older and at the end of their useful working life is because it takes years, decades really, to face such a variety of challenges and issues that one has the confidence to untangle a thorny issue objectively. This is the arena, more than a lot of others, where experience counts. Also, while the qualities that distinguish those who can add value on boards are similar, the styles are wildly different. And so it is a master class in interacting with an array of personalities and characters . . . some of whom might surprise you. Getting to know them outside of the boardroom is very rewarding. I worked with one Indian gentleman who, inside the boardroom, was tough as nails and suffered no fools. But one night when he and I shared a nightcap at the end of a long day, he told me that as a child, his parents sent him to the school in India where Mother Teresa worked and that he helped her after school for a few hours each day for years. As I asked him about her and he remembered his childhood memories, he became quite emotional. It was a side of him I had never seen. And that is just one example of the astounding experiences one can have swimming in this pool of talent!

And finally, boards meet in a variety of places and so there is an exposure to places (in addition to people) that you would never have access to under usual business circumstances. And, yes, the pay is attractive—usually a combination of cash and stock which, depending on how healthy the company is and how well the stock does, can certainly create some personal wealth.

But there is another side to the work that a lot of people either don't realize, or discount. The role is "cushy" until it's not. A crisis can happen anytime, usually very unexpectedly, and suddenly what had been four meetings a year can turn into weekly or even daily meetings. All aspects of your life go on hold—vacations get canceled; other commitments get deprioritized.

Take for example an experience I had many years ago on one of my boards. I was audit chair at the time and got a call from the CEO on New Year's Day. His voice was shaky and he was quite upset. In closing the books they had found a $40 million discrepancy in inventory values. They had no idea how or what had happened. Having somewhat of a forensic background, given my turnaround experience, I knew we had to diagnose the underlying cause. I looped in another member of the committee who was strong in accounting and we ended up traveling to the company and working out of a conference room for days to help determine the cause—the entire finance team and some outside advisors were working as well. I don't mean to imply that he and I single-handedly took this on. At the end of the day the cause was a "perfect storm" of both human error and bad timing: There was an IT transition to a new system going on and when a smaller discrepancy had appeared earlier, it was disregarded as the new IT system not working properly yet. By the time the installation was complete at the end of the following quarter, inventory valuations had changed significantly and the value of the gap had grown exponentially. In the end a restatement was necessary; most of the people in the company lost their bonuses that year and several people were terminated. Not pretty—and not easy to figure out. It took a while.

And consider several high-profile governance failures and the havoc that ensued for those companies. Two that immediately come to mind would be the BP oil spill in 2010 and the McDonald's succession crisis in 2004.

The BP oil spill is considered the largest marine oil spill in the history of the petroleum industry. But as terrible as that was, the spill was not the governance crisis—the spill was an operational failure. It was the CEO's response to the media, given while he was on a luxury vacation, that desecrated the company's reputation. First he said publicly that the spill was "relatively tiny in a very big ocean." After that he lamented that he would "like his life back," resentful of the intrusion on his personal time. He came to personify the disaster, and stands as a warning of the impact that bad management can have for decades after a crisis. Board members were tasked with rebuilding trust in the brand.

For McDonald's, two CEOs turned over in the course of seven months—the first died in a rafting accident and the second resigned when he was diagnosed with terminal cancer. That board needed an emergency succession plan and a longer-term CEO solution quickly.

In both cases those boards were faced with megasized operational and PR problems to solve.

Today, Boeing stands out as an example of a company whose board is facing a reputational crisis and I'm sure they are having to deal with a myriad of concerns and issues, requiring a huge time commitment.

I would also point to the COVID years when board meetings (on Zoom of course) *really* ratcheted up—crises abounded and even companies that were on the "winning" side of COVID's impact on business had immense challenges with supply chain issues and earnings unpredictability. And that doesn't even scratch the surface of the health risks and human resource issues that were unlike anything any of us had ever seen before. Most boards spent many hours for months working their way through the COVID time period. My crisis background has never come more in handy!

There is also a level of personal accountability when you are a director of a company. Everything is public—your background, your earnings, and your role on the board—and therefore what you personally can be held accountable for. At the very least, this means that shareholders can withhold votes for you if they do not like the results that they see. At the very worst, you could have some personal liability and a significant amount of reputational risk if bad things happen.

Consider the board of Wells Fargo—when incentive plans put in place at lower levels of the organization led people to open false accounts and create imaginary clients. Once the company reported this to the press, the shareholders went after the board. But the board is not responsible for incentive plans—or any compensation—below the senior executives, and so would have had no knowledge pertaining to incentive plans for lower ranks. Nevertheless—most of the outside world doesn't know (or care) about those nuances. Those directors took a beating reputationally.

Turning to the more mundane aspects of the boardroom role, a board operates as an entity of peers. Even the chairman—elected by his or her peers—doesn't have more power than any other director. They are simply charged with organizing and leading the board from an administrative perspective. Discourse and disagreement is never resolved by an authority figure higher than the directors. For better or worse, all decisions have to be wrestled to the ground by a group of people collectively.

One of my boards was created when two retail giants—and previous competitors—merged. Both CEOs were terminated as part of the merger. Five individuals from each of the prior boards were selected to move onto the newly created board. But the companies were wildly different in almost every way. There were (at the time) two headquarters—one in the North, one in the South. The corporate cultures were vastly different from each other. And the decisions that needed to be made—including hiring a new CEO—were daunting. In the beginning every vote was five to five, with no one to break the tie. It took a long time for that board to integrate and become fully functioning. But it evolved and eventually performed admirably.

I will note that sometimes the boardroom feels like high school! No matter how successful people are they still have their personality idiosyncrasies, their insecurities, and their personal prejudices. Not everyone gets along and—like high school—sometimes there are cliques and "more popular" and "less popular" directors.

And if you think all of that is worth thinking about before you get involved—please appreciate the CEO who not only has to run a company and deal with employees, shareholders, vendors, and investors, but who literally reports to roughly a dozen bosses! Communication and hand-holding from the CEO to the board takes an amazing amount of time ... and patience, I'm told (sometimes loudly).

Car Theft

I was on a private company board for a period of time that had operations in the Dominican Republic and Puerto Rico. Our board meetings were held in either San Juan or Santo Domingo. This particular meeting was held in Santo Domingo.

The local culture there is for late and long dinners—usually consisting of many courses and lasting late into the night. After the meeting ended, we headed to one of those long, late dinners, and some of us had early flights out the next morning. Our hotel was also quite a ways away from the restaurant where we were dining.

My friend and colleague, Nathan, whispered to me that we should just head back to the hotel because we both had to get up around four a.m. to get to the airport. The CEO suggested we take one of the corporate cars that we had valeted and made arrangements for us to return it in the morning near the airport. We made our excuses and left.

We were driving back to the hotel and chatting when we both started receiving calls from the CEO. Now, this CEO tended to be a little overprotective of board members and the two of us had never gone off on our own like that before, so we thought he was just checking up on us. But the calls kept coming and so finally one of us picked up.

He sounded very upset and told us we had taken someone else's car (the valet brought us the wrong one) and that that patron was extremely upset and threatening to call the police because his car had been stolen! Well—the chat ended abruptly and we high-tailed it back to the restaurant and attempted to soothe the ruffled feathers—and save the poor valet's job.

Needless to say, it was quite a late night, despite trying to leave early.

18

The Board Walk

"Landing a board role is hard. For most of us, it will be way harder than landing any job we've ever achieved."

—Athena Alliance

The million-dollar question these days is "How do I get on a board?"

It's not easy and, as we've already covered, it's not for everyone. And sadly, there are a lot of people who aspire to be on boards who just aren't qualified. To start with, some boardroom exposure is a must. And because of that, C-suite executives and CEOs are the most attractive candidates. They have been in the room, they have worked with the various committees, and they have presented to and fielded questions from directors within that setting, so it is not as intimidating for them as it is for the average bear. And a working knowledge of public company requirements, and exposure to and experience with all of the regulatory requirements, is a must.

That doesn't mean that it is impossible for others to play a role on a board. But it is a longer shot and typically that individual would have a very specific or special skill that the nominating committee of that board decided it was critical to have. Even that can be dicey—because most specific technical experience can be bought in the form of outside consulting or advisory services so that boards can gain access to the technical elements they think they need without using a board seat to get it. This is what had happened for the most part with cybersecurity.

About a decade ago a lot of boards considered putting a cyber expert on the board because the risk was so great and the threat was so real. (It still is.) However, the field of cybersecurity changes continually and it is hard to find one person who can consistently bring knowledge of all of the various elements about it to the boardroom. Also, it is technically management's job to protect the company from cyberattacks—it's the board's role to *govern* over that. And so very few boards ended up using a board seat to get access to that area of expertise.

Bear in mind that it is *very* hard to get rid of a director once they have been invited to join the board. I am sorry to say that even at this very high level in the corporate world, too often underperforming individuals are tolerated and are rarely actively encouraged to leave. These are hard conversations to have (I know; I've had them several times), and people get offended and feelings get bruised. Despite the fact that board evaluations have come a long way—and now a number of boards do peer-to-peer assessments—real, direct feedback is still lacking in many cases because people want to be nice to each other. Yet, 49 percent of directors feel that there is at least one member on their board who should go. It is one of the reasons why some consider the boardroom out of date and not representative of the greater population. The adage is "male, pale, and stale." I truly believe that we need a mechanism to retain the highest-performing directors and graciously honor—and replace—those whose time it is to leave. And I fervently wish that more directors would have the self-awareness and generosity to offer up their seat when the time comes.

There is also some patience involved with finding a board seat. It is a unique hiring process, unlike the typical process to get an executive job. Interviews are largely conducted by the search firm until the top one or two candidates are surfaced and then those candidates will interview with several board members. But that process can take months. And often, unforeseen circumstances occur and the board may call off the search. Or, even more frustrating, the search continues but they ran out of time at the board meeting to discuss it, so it gets punted to the next board meeting months later. It is arduous.

I would also add that too many executives, when interviewing for their first board, do not understand how to do the interview for a board seat—simply because it *is* such a completely different role than that of active management. As a director, you do not have responsibility for any of the operations of the company. So the interview will not be about what you have done in the past from a leadership perspective—remember, this is a group of peers! The questions—and more importantly, the answers—need to show several things that display a working knowledge of the role of the board. Answers should be about strategic insight and the ability to ask the right questions to gain understanding about a complex issue. They should also demonstrate the ability to influence as a peer—to confidently express a point of view that may be counter to what your peers say—albeit to do it professionally and compellingly (and briefly). Cultural fit is paramount—so read the room, display strong EQ, and make sure to ask insightful and probing questions about the company, the board, and the CEO dynamics.

I was approached for the first time about a board seat just after the turn of the century, and it happened through the age-old informal network that exists in the business world. I was just starting my crisis CFO work at the CFO firm. A company that was out of state approached their outside counsel looking for a board member with financial expertise. But here's the serendipity of it: The CEO of the company supported adding a board member with a financial background, but he added another search criteria—he requested that the board find a mom of young kids to take the slot. He reasoned that his boardroom was populated with older (mostly) men and the company's product was targeted to moms and kids.

"Bring me someone who looks and thinks like my consumer," he said.

They put the word out, and eventually the request came into the CFO firm and Dirk said that yes, in fact, he had someone who fit that description. I flew out to interview for that board seat absolutely positive there was no way in hell I was going to get it—I was probably about ten years too early in my career to be considered for such a thing. A week or so after the interview, I got the call and they offered it to me. I was shocked—and excited—and scared. I was *so* proud of myself, and surprised that things had worked out so well. It turns out I really liked being a board member, and from that first seat came many others in the years to come—so much so that I was able to retire much earlier than expected and switch to just being a professional board member.

And this was a "life is stranger than fiction" moment as well. For one thing—at that point in time, moms did not really flaunt their childcare responsibilities for fear that bosses would be concerned about their ability to perform. This meant my kids weren't exactly a topic at work very often. How ironic then that my children were the vehicle through which I was able to make such a profound professional jump—and one that has truly transformed my work life and become my passion. But the kicker? It turns out I didn't "win" the job at all ... they simply couldn't find any other woman with small kids who was crazy enough to be a public company CFO!

The last thing that I would say is that in every single case—and don't believe anyone who tells you otherwise—there is an element of luck involved. I liken it to an actor's pursuit of stardom ... I believe that there are many more talented actors than there are roles. How many more Meryl Streeps or Tom Cruises are out there who just never had that "right" audition or that lucky break? You need to network, connect, and tell everyone that you can that you want a board seat ... but then you also need to be in the right place at the right time for it to come to fruition. If the CEO of my first board hadn't wanted a mom on his board, I never would have been considered. If my CFO firm had not had an intracompany site for posting, the board seat in Colorado would never have been visible to my boss in Chicago for me to become a candidate. And had they found anyone else who qualified for the position—well, I might not have been selected. Believe me, there is some providence involved with getting into this "club."

If you are trying to get on a board, bear these statistics in mind: According to David Schwarz, who runs Board Appointments, 65 percent of board seats come through a personal or professional connection, 15 percent from a direct approach from the company, and only 10 percent through recruiters. About the same amount, 10 percent, come from an advertisement or posting. So work your network!

With all of that said, stop and evaluate and really think about whether or not a director role is a good fit for you. Here are the characteristics about it that I really think one should consider:

- *The job is inherently unpredictable—and you do not have any ability to influence that.*

- *You will have no direct responsibility for results—if you are a hands-on or high-control person, that will drive you crazy.*

- *It requires restraint, patience, high EQ, and great communication skills.*

- *It requires a backbone—you may take a stand that is unpopular.*

- *You can't have thin skin. Other board members, management, investors, and even the press will have the ability to pass judgment on you.*

- *Sometimes your brain will hurt from the complexities of the issues that you will deal with.*

As noted, my journey to the boardroom was remarkably lucky. That first board came as a result of the CEO wanting a mom to represent his consumer. Not only was that very specific, but the randomness of their attorney passing that on to a Denver person affiliated with my CFO firm, who then posted it on the company site, was fortuitous. If any one of those connections hadn't happened, I would not have been ushered into my next career. And believe me, a CEO wanting that kind of customer intimacy is pretty common now but wasn't back then.

And my lucky streak continued. It turns out, organic food products which the company produced have a cult-like following, and when my press release came out for joining that first board, the chairman of the nominating committee at another company took note (his daughter being a natural food chef) and he wrote me a snail-mail letter to the company; the company then forwarded that letter to me at my home address asking me if I would be interested in interviewing for a second board in a completely different industry. Again, what are the chances? If that letter hadn't been forwarded to me—or had been forwarded incorrectly—or if I had simply ignored it, then that opportunity wouldn't have materialized—and I was on that board for twenty-one years!

Ready for the third stroke of dumb luck? We sold the organic food company about two-and-a-half years after I joined the board; luckily I was able to make a handsome profit (which, by the way, allowed me to pay for my oldest son's college . . . something I had been stressing about for years). The bankers who completed the deal for us hosted a closing party at the top of a mountain at a charming restaurant in Colorado. The mood was celebratory and the altitude affected everyone to magnify both the alcohol and the mood! Side note—I have since learned that I react to altitude much worse than the average person and so I now avoid traveling above 7,500 feet. But at the time, it was a great party and a happy night.

Coming back down the mountain, we had to ride in snowcats to get to the bottom, where the hotel was, and I ended up riding back down with two of the bankers. It was only about a ten-minute ride, but in that time, they told me that they were taking a company public and asked if I would be interested in interviewing to become audit committee chair post-IPO. I *was* interested and I *did* become audit chair and remained on that board for ten years.

When I tell you there is luck involved, I mean it. Any traditional recruiter would have looked at my résumé, my age, and my inexperience and never would have presented me for those opportunities. And, in fact, it was over a decade later, once I was on several boards in leadership roles, before the more traditional recruiters took an interest in me and my phone started ringing.

Nevertheless, within three years of getting that first board, I had experience with three boards and I actively served on two of them as audit chair for at least the next ten years. And so by 2006 I was balancing my turnaround CFO career, raising my sons, and sitting on two public company boards until I retired in 2013. Yes, I was busy. But I had some control over my schedule in terms of what CFO jobs

I took on, I had a great support system for my kids, and the boards stayed on a pretty regular cadence most of the time. That is not to say there weren't occasional crises in any of those three areas from time to time ... but not at the same time, thankfully, and—after all—I was trained and experienced in crisis management at this point!

While I may have stumbled into my first three board seats, I did not fail to recognize the serendipity that got me there and I never stopped appreciating those opportunities that came my way. I was "all in" in terms of learning the board role, actively participating in all ways, both inside and outside the boardroom. What does that mean? It means going above and beyond to learn about the company. I sought out time with senior management to learn about all aspects of the business. I read every SEC filing front to back; I visited stores, distribution centers, and plants. It also meant investing in my board education, and I attended various outside programs in order to strengthen my understanding and knowledge. And it meant getting to know and building relationships with my fellow board members. I dove in and—while that effort probably started from a feeling of impostor syndrome—over time and as I got comfortable in my role, I realized that I loved the work and that it fit me perfectly.

You Can't Come In

Board meetings are very stressful for the management team and especially for the CEO. There is a tremendous amount of buildup, preparation, and rehearsal. Various ideas come up for formal approval, many of which the CEO views as instrumental to his ability to attain the desired results. Board meetings are also typically pretty close to, if not immediately preceding, the quarterly earnings release and an intense period of interaction with shareholders. Most CEOs I know breathe a sigh of relief when all of it is over and they can get back to day-to-day operations. Having not one but a roomful of bosses that you interact with for two straight days can't be fun.

But it could be worse. What if you did all of the preparation and then couldn't attend the actual meeting?

In one of the first boards I ever joined, we received a whistleblower complaint—anonymously submitted—the morning of the board meeting and brought only to the chairman's attention. It involved someone accusing the CEO of removing documents critical to the financial audit, which was occurring at the time, from the premises. Allegedly, he was observed putting documents in his car and leaving with them.

It is not unusual for anonymous complaints of various sorts to come in—and companies actively promote this as a "safe" way for employees to report problems. The vast majority of them—by a longshot—relate to lower-level HR issues or ethical breaches (like petty theft) that can be easily researched and resolved. Rarely do they relate to the CEO and very few make it to the board for resolution.

And so this was weird—and the timing of it was particularly strange. The fact that it came in the morning of the board meeting meant we had to take immediate action. So the chairman assembled the meeting earlier than planned and communicated the issue. The group of us knew that we needed to do an investigation into the CEO.

So when the CEO showed up at the regularly scheduled meeting time, he was told he was not allowed in the room! And I am not sure how this snafu happened, but I learned later that he had no idea why and was not informed of the actual accusation until days later. He must have been so confused!

The end to the story is very straightforward—the investigation showed that he had left with materials on the date in question—but they were merely marketing materials that he wanted to review at home that night. There was nothing untoward happening and someone either mistook his intent or, worse, had it out for him and used the anonymous reporting option to do it. We never knew because we never knew who that person was.

But even though it all worked out in the end, it was one of the strangest things I've ever witnessed in a boardroom—a CEO thrown out of his own meeting. I asked that CEO years later what that experience had been like for him, thinking it must have been very upsetting and memorable. Incredibly, I had to remind him what I was even talking about—and when I did he said, "Well, I knew I'd done nothing wrong, so I didn't give it a second thought!" ... Cool as a cucumber, that one!

19

Making Herstory

"After a while I looked in the mirror and realized ... wow, after all those hurts, scars, and bruises, after all of those trials, I really made it through. I did it. I survived that which was supposed to kill me. So I straightened my crown ... and walked away like a boss."

—Anonymous

I eventually set my sights on becoming a full-time board member and began to consider retiring from the CFO career track. It was a slow evolution over a number of years and I was unsure if I could actually do it—because even at this point, most traditional recruiters were not contacting me for new board roles. But, remembering my year off earlier in my career and my lessons in patience, having faith that things tend to work themselves out, and remembering the resilience muscle I had built up, I decided in 2013 to officially retire. I still had my two boards, and since that was the year my youngest son graduated from high school, I found myself by September of that year as an empty nester with so much more time on my hands that I truly didn't know what to do with myself! Reminding myself not to panic, I took full advantage of the opportunity to move south into a rented condo near my elderly parents for the winter and tried to relax.

Sure enough, in 2014, I was contacted by Starboard Value because they were interested in interviewing me to be a proposed director candidate in a proxy fight involving a consumer retail business. It was a well-known brand. But even though I had been hoping to interview for another board, I was hesitant. Activists take a stock position in companies that have depressed results and then pressure management to make changes. Usually those changes involve both corporate strategy and corporate governance. In other words, usually they want to rethink the business model *and* replace at least some directors.

Activism is a broad term and there are a lot of firms who do it with a lot of different styles and approaches. The most aggressive and abusive ones usually make the headlines, but like I learned firsthand, there are also many constructive activists who truly want what is best for the shareholders. Over the years since my first exposure, I have been on both sides of the activism wave. I have been an activist-appointed director and I have defended against aggressive and not-so-nice activists. I have served *as* an activist director and I have served *with* activist directors. Back then this was all new ... although joining a board through an activist has become very mainstream these days, after a decade or more of campaigns involving some of the most recognizable companies.

But in 2014, activism was a new practice that was not particularly well regarded. I hesitated because I was concerned with becoming known as an activist director, which implied a few concerning things. For one, folks wonder if you are "in the pocket" of the activist ... will they tell you what to do and how to vote? And would it mean that you are not attractive as a traditional candidate? Will it preclude you from getting other boards through a traditional route in the future because you are branded? It was definitely a high-risk career move at that time.

Jeff Smith started Starboard Value. His staff do the initial phases of identifying and interviewing board candidates. In this case, I put them off a few times. But I came to appreciate their persistence because when I met with Jeff, I really appreciated that he wanted to hear my thoughts about the business. He appreciated my turnaround skills and background, and he didn't strike me as a person who would expect obedience in exchange for the board seat. So I signed on—but even then it was a longshot. Activist campaigns rarely go all the way to a formal proxy fight because most companies want to spare that distraction and expense. Therefore, they usually negotiate with the activist and try to reduce the number of board seats up for grabs. In this case, Jeff wanted six seats but settled for three. And since he had six candidates, he could choose between us to decide which three he wanted to put on that board.

I had mixed feelings at the time when I learned I had been selected. But it turned into a great experience and I stayed on that board for a long time—long after Jeff had exited and I had proven myself as having an independent mind in the boardroom.

As a matter of fact, a few years later I worked with Jeff again and joined a second board through his sponsorship. Since this is public, I feel I can share the experience of joining the complete turnover of the Darden Board in 2014. It is well known that Starboard Value successfully replaced the entire prior board after waging an activist campaign against them, claiming bad governance and offering alternative views on how to better create shareholder value. This was unprecedented at the time, and I believe it still is today. By the time I was asked to participate, there had already been some back and forth between the company and Starboard; the interactions, from what I understand, were heated and not particularly productive. They also became quite public over time after Starboard published a two-hundred-plus-page document pointing out a number of areas where the board and the company could improve. (John Oliver gave a scathing and quite funny bit about it on his show at the time—it is worth looking it up online!)

Starboard had originally asked for some (not complete) board representation, but as the dialogue continued and things devolved, they demanded more until the "ask" was for shareholders to vote to replace the entire board. I was one of the fourteen new directors proposed in the proxy fight. It was a real longshot at the time, but the momentum really built and it became clear within a few days of the formal meeting that the shareholder vote would be in favor of the Starboard slate. That left the fourteen of us to walk into a room of shareholders, media, employees, and various outside advisors to formally assume our new responsibilities. We had very tight security and each of us was assigned a bodyguard throughout the meeting. It was surreal.

But that was just the beginning.

Imagine fourteen virtual strangers walking into an empty board-room together for the first time and having to sort out, well, *everything*! Leadership roles, committee assignments, working relationships, and priorities. As strange as it was for us, I know it was even worse for the executives who had to come into that room and present, especially given the perceived hostility leading up to the changeover. It was a strange and dramatic lesson in governance at its most extreme.

While it eventually normalized over time and both the size of the board and the functionality of the board improved, it was interest-ing for so many reasons: the crazy media coverage, the experience of becoming an activist director, and the fun of watching that company rebound and thrive under new management. Again, that proved to be a great opportunity and one that has lasted. If there is any lesson in that, it is about taking chances and embracing untraditional routes to gain new opportunities.

* * *

Once in the boardroom, regardless of how you got there, you have to be prepared for anything. Every board is different and each board has its own character. I have been on boards that were divided and con-tentious. I have been on boards that struggled to take a united stand. Some have had great relationships with the management teams; some have been splintered. Many have had factions. All have had a wide range of personalities. And the companies that we govern are equally diverse. Some have stupendous success. Many struggle. The vagaries of capitalist markets can make for wild cyclical swings, and the reg-ulatory environment has changed dramatically over the time that I have been in boardrooms. Consider the many societal episodes that have occurred since I joined my first board in the early 2000s:

- Sarbanes-Oxley Act—a sweeping regulatory change by Congress to try to better protect against fraud after Enron, Tyco, and WorldCom. It exponentially increased the amount of work that finance teams and audit committees had to do to ensure that internal controls were in place to protect assets.

- The dot-com boom and bust of the early 2000s, when internet company valuations of early-stage companies and M&A deals involving those kinds of companies peaked and then crashed.

- The real estate bubble burst and the Great Recession followed. Raising capital became very difficult and a lot of smaller companies went out of business.

- Both Trump presidencies, with the wild and unpredictable tariffs threatened, applied, and sometimes rescinded, wreaked havoc on international trade.

- The ascendancy of social media, with all of its transparency as well as its disinformation, can impact a company literally overnight.

- The COVID years, when every workplace was severely disrupted and supply chains were constrained, paralyzed the movement of goods and services globally and drove up persistent inflation.

- And today, the geopolitical unrest in the Middle East and Ukraine, the rise of right-wing nationalism, and the political polarity and instability in the US (and elsewhere) continue to impact supply chains and trade policies.

All of these are deeply felt in the boardroom and drive conversations and decisions that can swing wildly depending on each company's unique circumstances. The rate and pace of change and the decision-making surrounding it requires boards and board members to stay on top of things, to think through the potential opportunities and pitfalls, and to strive to best represent the interests of the shareholders.

As I write this in the summer of 2024, one of the companies where I am a director is facing an existential crisis due to shifting market dynamics and depressed consumer demand. It will likely file for restructuring. The management team has fought so valiantly and has done all of the right things to try to stem the tide. But sometimes macroeconomic forces are just too strong to overcome, and the burden of fixed costs is just too high. In this case it is heartbreaking—yet in the end, restructuring and selling to a private equity firm (called a "stalking horse") at least keeps the business going and saves the jobs of thousands of workers. The shareholder may not win, unfortunately, but the employees and vendors will survive and that is important. It is the silver lining after a hard-fought struggle.

At this point, I would say I have a high level of knowledge of corporate governance. And having been in this role for over twenty years, I feel like I have seen just about everything. The companies I have had board seats on span a wide range of industries, from media and manufacturing to retail and consumer products. The sizes range from start-up to a market cap of $28 billion. In my twenty years I have been chairman of three public company boards and one private board, five audit committees, two corporate governance committees, and one compensation committee. I have been involved with five CEO searches (and a few exits); I have led six special investigations related to a variety of (alleged) wrongdoing at the executive level, and I have been on special committees related to everything from a CEO medical emergency to executing merger agreements to defending shareholder lawsuits. It has certainly been a wild ride and it has never been boring!

Let's talk about being the chair of a board—it is a completely different and unique kind of leadership role. For one thing, you are elected by your peers but you are still only one vote on any issue. It is a "first among equals" scenario where you have more responsibility but not necessarily more power. The duties of the chair have mostly to do with communication, organization, and building consensus. The chair has the closest relationship with the CEO. Part consigliere, part gentle critic and bearer of bad news, and part punching bag, the role is always a challenge. Within the boardroom, you set agendas, keep the meeting on track, and routinely check in with each board member to make sure that their views are heard. Sometimes, there is some level of hand-holding involved. Sometimes, you mediate disagreements. Honestly, it isn't that different from parenting in some ways!

I wish I could share a few "war stories" from my boardroom years, but that would either violate confidentiality or would be doing a disservice to the many terrific directors and boards out there that are highly functioning and extremely effective. Those are boards at their best. What a feeling of accomplishment to wrestle a thorny issue to the ground, gain concurrence, and later watch the results confirm that you acted appropriately! But like any endeavor dependent on human interaction, of course there can be "stranger than fiction" episodes.

I will offer this: I have seen irate CEOs so furious at their board that fists almost flew. I have seen drunk directors and senile directors. I have been hit on by other directors. I have seen directors attack one another verbally, and I have seen directors become quite emotional at times.

Each and every time I took on a leadership role within the boardroom, it was after having to advocate for myself, which is awkward and hard for me. Mostly, the initially nominated candidates were men. So some of that bias still exists, even at the top. Per Equileap's 2024 *Gender Equality Report & Ranking*, out of nearly 1,600 US companies, only 9 percent have a woman as chair of the board—despite women making up 30 percent of the boards in the US (which is still an abysmally low percentage). Listen to this: In the top 1,000 public US companies, there are more male CEOs named John or David than there are total female CEOs! So it shouldn't surprise anyone that I have been interrupted, talked over, and mansplained to so many times I've lost count. I've been "confused" with another woman on the board (as if we're all interchangeable!). And of course, there are times where my "great idea" is ignored until a man says it, at which point it is warmly embraced. It certainly doesn't happen all the time; it doesn't even happen anywhere nearly as frequently now as in the past ... but it still does happen.

And I have also felt deeply respected and valued. I have built lasting relationships with wonderful peers. I have fought through confusing times and scary times and bad times in the company of "soldiers I would choose to be in the foxhole with." I have learned, oh have I learned, about leadership and courage and integrity. I have felt every emotion you could possibly feel from giddiness and excitement, to fear and despair, to curiosity and confusion. I have laughed so hard my sides hurt and have been bursting with pride when I watch a plan come together and a management team win.

I know the boardroom stands for a wide range of things to different people. For some it is a bastion of greedy capitalism, preserving the power structure of yesteryear. For others it is a career aspiration and goal. For many it is a mysterious entity so foreign and disconnected from their day-to-day life that they rarely think about it with any feeling at all. For me, it has been my Disneyland and my Hades. My mountaintop and my gutter. My best and my worst. My learning lab and my playground. I can't wait to keep going!

Push and Pull

There are all kinds of reasons a company could need a turnaround CFO, but most involve urgency and crisis. Such was definitely the case when I became the CFO for a private insurance brokerage firm where the senior management team had turned the CEO in to the DOJ for the inappropriate use of client funds.

As with all brokerages, when client funds are paid into the brokerage, but are not yet disbursed to the carriers, they are required to be held in a separate trust account and not touched. In this case, the CEO played a little fast and loose with those funds, which I honestly think probably happens from time to time in that industry. The genesis of the claim, however, turned out to have more to do with hubris and revenge. That CEO had been promising his senior team a share of ownership in the company for years and had never come through. Their resentment built and anger boiled over into a "we'll get you" kind of groupthink.

They made the call and unleashed a tsunami. The DOJ immediately raided the company and the CEO and CFO were terminated. In this case, the CEO was also the owner and so there was a strange arrangement where he lived nearby and was free until trial, but was not allowed to have any management "influence or input" into the company's operations. The trial took about two years to begin. Ultimately, he went to prison. In the meantime, he freely wandered the halls and made himself a general nuisance to all of us trying to carry on.

After the indictment, they needed to constitute a board (primarily composed of various lawyers) and select an internal CEO and CFO. They chose one of the senior guys in the company—not involved in the accusation—and offered him the COO role (they were preserving the CEO role for the owner who, at that point, expressed great confidence that he would be back), and they approached my CFO firm to find an emergency CFO. I was selected.

It quickly became apparent to me that the newly constituted board had two factions—one that thought the CEO was innocent and continually fed boardroom decisions back to him, and the other side that thought the faster this went to trial the better, and were very supportive of the DOJ.

To this day it was the strangest work environment I have ever experienced. The previous CFO's computer had been confiscated and the financial records were in disarray. I remember walking into the supply closet and finding an open box of checks located right next to the ink signature stamp. No internal controls whatsoever! In addition, I was duly warned—the feds had the office phones and the offices themselves bugged, so everything I did was under surveillance. On a fairly frequent basis, the disgraced CEO would wander into my office to "chat." When he did so, he would always direct his voice to the ceiling. (Clearly he was communicating with the DOJ, not with me.)

Most of my role consisted of making sure we improved and relied on effective internal controls so that all transactions were squeaky clean. I also had to prepare for and present in numerous board meetings—they seemed to be called on very short notice and very frequently so that servicing the board took most of my time. I tried to keep my presentations very fact-based so as not to get in between the two factions on the board, which was becoming increasingly dysfunctional.

In one meeting, however, I had prepared a book so that folks could follow along as I took them through some intricate financial analyses. At the end, I always collected my presentations back so that the highly confidential nature of the materials could not be breached. In this case, one of the directors, who was the most closely aligned with the accused CEO, refused to give me his copy. I asked politely several times. He refused. I acted on impulse (perhaps not the smartest impulse), and I went around to his side of the table and tried to grab the book. He resisted and we ended up in a push-and-pull kind of back and forth that I'm sure was quite entertaining. He was about six feet, five inches tall and well over two hundred pounds and he had stood up. He towered over me. But I was not going to let go! This seemed to continue forever—but I'm sure it was probably thirty seconds or less.

Eventually—finally—the acting chairman intervened and told him to give me the book back. I have no idea why it had to come to that—but I will say that my decision to fight for the book, literally, cemented my reputation as not one to mess with for the remainder of my time there.

And So . . .

Yes, it all looks so easy from the outside. But it is *not* easy from the inside. Choosing to learn and grow and play and suffer and endeavor in the workplace is not easy. Still, the corporate world really just mirrors the broader world and is just one arena where we play this game called life. Each person has the choice to make it what they will, and not everyone chooses to play the game in this particular arena. But in the end, we all learn the lessons we need to learn. The lessons learned are life lessons. The personalities encountered can be Shakespearean. Stakes are high and egos can be even higher. It takes guts, grit, and persistence to stay. But I found it so worth it.

Over the decades—through the jobs, the bosses, the failures, the successes, the promotions, and the setbacks—I grew. I grew stronger, I built confidence, and I rebounded from trauma—as each of us has to learn to do in this life. I became a leader through trial and error. I made the decision to learn from the terrible bosses that I had as well as the good ones. It is all instructional. I bear no grudges. All of my experiences provided the opportunity to become better.

I am so fortunate that my journey eventually took me to a place where I can have an impact as a leader. I can advocate for positive change and I can directly impact corporate strategy for the better. I know that I am a survivor, and as such, I feel the responsibility to share my experiences and my truth. I really want to help others as so many others helped me. If I can demystify it, and help even one person struggling to understand where they are and how they fit and what they can do to be better/happier, than all of it was worth it.

Still, I wish I had been more prepared. I wish there had been classes—in my MBA or in my corporate training—that could have been provided to better prepare me for the challenges to come. If I could write a "Corporate Survival Guide" it would include:

- How to Assess a Job Opportunity

- Influencing Up, Down, and Across

- Surviving Toxic Environments

- Mastering High-EQ Leadership

- Embracing Change

- Assessing Ethical Dilemmas

- Balancing Priorities

- Understanding the Power of Courage

My journey was obviously a time and place story set mostly in the late 1980s to the present. A lot has changed—but some general themes can still transcend my time and place. Unfortunately, there will always be bad bosses and toxic work environments. The push for profits will usually trump human resource issues. Human nature—with all of its foibles—will not change. And it is up to each one of us to take agency around all of that and play our parts with authenticity and integrity.

I am struck by what an extraordinary position I had in the unique combination of being a woman, a single mom, a turnaround CFO, a chairman of the board, and—at times—a failure. I had so many perspectives! So many opportunities! So many experiences—what a privilege. I feel I can identify with all of the challenges unique to each of those. And it is my mission to somehow blend all of those together as I strive in my small way to make the business world better. I will keep trying.

I will advocate for equality and opportunity. For diversity and for corporate social responsibility—even as the pressure to pull back on such things builds. I want us to move forward, not backward. I know I sit in rarified air. I know how hard it was to get here.

I promise not to waste it.

My Bucket List

- [ ] Change someone's life
- [ ] Do something that scares you
- [ ] Stand up for yourself
- [ ] Give someone a second chance
- [ ] Learn something new
- [ ] Be curious about something
- [ ] Treat yourself
- [ ] Change a bad habit (or start a good one)
- [ ] Refrain from giving someone advice
- [ ] Exhibit patience in a trying situation

Acknowledgments

I would like to thank first every boss I've ever had . . . the blood, sweat, tears, paranoia, and anxiety that you all caused eventually led to this book. I would also like to thank the fraught election of 2024 for providing so much frustration and angst that diving into my past through writing provided the best escape from the present.

There are a lot of people who contributed to and encouraged this undertaking. First and foremost, Jenniffer Weigel, who taught me so much, grounded my approach, adjusted my thinking, and traded endless versions of drafts with great review notes and suggestions. This would never have happened without you! Several other people who also came into my life to guide this book from idea to publication and were instrumental: Jennifer Geist, John St. Augustine, and Julie Wilson—thank you!

To my peers on the boards that I have been on—you have been inspirational and have taught me so much—thank you for modeling good governance. A special shout-out to Pete Braud, George MacKenzie, Mark Weikel, Wendy Schoppert, Kristin Campbell, Nancy Reardon, and Tom Kingsbury. To the CEOs I have worked closely with as chair—Hal, Greg, Bruce, Rick, and Jon—we have been through a lot of challenges; your leadership inspires me every day. And to the management teams supporting those CEOs—your hard work, dedication, and professionalism do not go unnoticed!

I'd also like to thank Jeff Smith for writing the foreword to this book—we have seen some things and I have learned a lot from you. I so appreciate the opportunities you gave me to further learn and grow

I owe a shout-out to the friends who over the years kept prompting me to write a book about the crazy experiences I've shared with them. Jeannette, Renee, Jennifer, Maureen, and DeAnn. Thank you for continuing to push me to do this—it was very cathartic!

To my wonderful sisters, Carol and Ginnie, the only birth family I have left. You guys are the best—always offering support and love when I need it.

To my "early readers"—I cannot thank you enough for showing interest, providing improvement ideas, and cheering me on! Thank you, Sarah King, Mark Cooper, Lauren Werle, Maya Tubic, Fraser Clark, Atlee Valentine-Pope, Zoe Maloney, Kevin Moffitt, Jane Howze, Betsy Zorio, Kimberly Simpson, Stacey Keller, and Cheryl Steffen. Also to my eternally proud and supportive husband for gracefully accepting *not* being asked to be an early reader . . . you encouraged me but stayed out of my way. And you did a *lot* of dog walks that should have been on my watch. You're the best!

And of course, most if not all of this book—the experiences, the stories, and the lessons—would not have happened if I hadn't been supporting and raising four amazing boys, now men. My eternal gratitude for having you in my life! Nicholas, Michael, Joshua, Ryan—you simultaneously made me insane and kept me sane at the same time. We not only survived—we thrived. I love you boys with all my heart.

About the Author

Cynthia Jamison ascended to the top echelons of corporate governance after a successful career as a turnaround CFO. With an undergraduate degree from Duke University and a master's in finance from the University of Chicago, she ascended through the financial world with jobs in banking, accounting, consumer products, professional services, and various other industries. She became a first-time public company CFO in 1999 at the age of 39. From there, she became a partner at an interim CFO equity partnership specializing in middle-market turnarounds. There she successfully led six different organizations (both public and private-equity backed) through turnarounds as either CFO or COO—eventually moving into a practice leadership role within the firm where she had three hundred-plus CFOs reporting to her. She elevated the profile of the firm through thought leadership initiatives which included keynote addresses to major financial audiences on topics such as the risks of the CFO role.

In 2009 she accepted one last CFO role at a small environmental start-up, secured equity funding for that company during the Great Recession of 2008–09, and built out the finance function. That company survives today, although Ms. Jamison formally retired as CFO in 2013. She remained on the board of directors until she recently stepped down, in part to focus on this book.

Ms. Jamison joined her first public company board of directors in 2002 and continued from there to build an impressive board portfolio. In the twenty-plus years since then, she has chaired four boards, three public and one private, and actively chairs one today. She has chaired five audit committees. She retired in 2023 as chairman of the board of Tractor Supply Company—one of the highest-performing stocks in this century—where she had served for twenty-one years. Today she serves on the boards of Darden Restaurants, Office Depot, and International Flavors & Fragrances.

Ms. Jamison recently completed a four-year term as a member of FASAC, the advisory board to the Financial Accounting Standards Board (FASB). In addition, she is an NACD Board Leadership Fellow and was awarded the honor of "Top 100 Director." She also sits on the board of Save the Children. She is a frequent keynote speaker on CFO and boardroom topics, and has been quoted as a financial/economic expert in *Forbes*, the *Wall Street Journal*, *Newsweek*, *CFO.com*, *Agenda*, *Corporate Board Member*, and the *Economist*.